En mi auto

por Sarah Holliday
ilustrado por Chris Van Dusen

 Harcourt

Orlando   Boston   Dallas   Chicago   San Diego

www.harcourtschool.com

El oso en mi auto.

 La tortuga en mi auto.

El yak en mi auto.

 La foca en mi auto.

5

El pulpo en mi auto.

El elefante en mi auto.

¡El elefante en mi auto!

VENOM
and STEEL

PROLOGUE

The Changeling

IN A THREE-ROOM SHACK DEEP WITHIN THE EASTERNMOST valleys slept a human babe. Its swaddling gown was thin, threadbare and secondhand, the color dull with age. To the young blue fey, the babe smelled like meat.

Fira giggled, tiptoeing across the uneven plank floor, and Fedrine, half again her size, pushed the fairy and hissed a warning to be silent. It was too rough, and the smaller fairy rolled forward in her stumble, crashing awkwardly—noisily—into the makeshift crib. The babe screamed and jolted to waking, and Fira covered her own ears as she cowered below.

Footsteps sounded in the main room.

Fedrine grabbed the swaddled child and tossed it, bundle and all, out the window. As it landed in the tall grass, Fira cried out in protest, her tiny hands gesturing through the air. Fedrine's eyes narrowed on the other fey, their depthless black inspiring both a spike of fear and the thrill of the hunt. He motioned toward the naked bedding.

Fira smiled then crawled into the youngling's crib.

When the humans entered their firstborn child's bedroom, it was not the slender form of Fedrine they saw. The changeling fey had shifted, his skin going pale, the fur lining his neck curling into long chestnut locks, kissed by the sun. His thin lips were softened and curved, and color dotted his cheeks. The only thing unchanged was the endless chasm of his eyes. His head tilted down, and his hand snaked slowly over the soft lumps of what appeared to be their unharmed babe in its bed. It would look to the humans like a blessing, some angel of mercy come to show favor upon their child.

The human woman fell to her knees, shaking as her work-calloused palms covered her mouth. "Heavens," she whispered through her bony fingers, as underfed as she was. "Heavens exalt us with this gift."

It was clear she was waiting for some response, but Fedrine did not speak. The changelings had no words.

The changelings had teeth.

FREY

IT HAD BEEN THREE SEASONS SINCE OUR RETURN TO THE CASTLE, three seasons of peace and rightness since the fey had last breached the walls. It figured that was all the peace we would be allowed.

"Where are they?" I demanded, grabbing my scabbard from the high table near the bedroom door.

Grey's dagger, sticky with blood, was already in his hand. "The east hall."

I cursed. We had barely finished renovations from their last late-night visit. "And Ruby?"

Grey took a breath but didn't answer. I hesitated, my chest clenching until his eyes met mine with a flicker of unidentifiable emotion. "I don't know," he said.

Then we ran through corridor after corridor until we met the massive, open chamber that was the east hall.

The walls were covered in fire. The stone burned with an unnatural green flame, popping and crackling while pale-skinned fey danced beneath its glow. There were seventeen of them. Six paraded across the uneven ledge where a window had once been, three were tangled in a violent argument that hovered over the far corner, and the rest were on foot before the slender few of my guard who were present.

I took stock of them, the seven whose duty was to protect me and to stand at my side during a fight. Chevelle and Rider had been gathering sentries south of the mountain and weren't expected back until midday. Steed and Rhys were there, though, parrying attacks from several frost monsters near the opposite wall while Grey and I fought our way to reach them.

Anvil and Ruby were nowhere in sight.

The small gathering of lesser fey was not what had me concerned. It was nearing dawn, and I knew what was to come. "Clear the hall," I screamed, "or so help me, I will break the treaty and scatter your pieces!"

A roar of cackling laughter rolled through the open chamber. The creatures were out for blood. My threats meant nothing. I wondered only briefly if they'd already secured some, if the guards on the outer walls had paid that price. It would have been enough reason to end them immediately, but there was more to come.

Another visitor would soon arrive, one who could not be so easily dispatched. We needed to secure Ruby from the fey.

"Find her," I told Steed and Rhys. "Whatever you do, don't let them take her."

They looked as if they wanted to argue, but our number in the hall would not change the outcome. Veil would arrive soon, and his only interest was me. I made it an order. "Now."

Steed drew a breath, purposefully catching my eye before he followed in Rhys's footsteps. Something had happened. There was more they were not telling me.

Because we didn't have time. Orange streaked the skyline, the strange glint of firelight making it seem unreal. We had minutes, maybe. There was nothing I could do. I glanced at Grey, wishing I could in some way use my power and connect to his magic the way I had to Chevelle's to keep the fey from manipulating it. "Where are the wolves?"

He returned my gaze, giving the smallest shake of his head —he didn't know.

The fey had been waiting. "They want me alone," I said.

Grey shifted closer. A thin, pale frost monster narrowed his focus on Grey's weapon.

"If they move in," I whispered, "spare no one." It wasn't a secret, and the fey were addicted to secrets. It was a warning that I knew they would hear and that I needed them to understand. The fey had been crossing to our lands, putting our people in danger. It had to stop.

The frost monster licked his ashen lips.

There was a crash in the hallway, followed by the clang and peal of metal. The sentries were dealing with their own nuisance, but they'd been warned to leave the high fey to my personal guard. The fey we were about to face would have been too dangerous for them.

A hiss of whispers rose through the eastern hall, their anticipation of the rising sun too much to contain. It gathered steam, pitching into riotous excitement. My palms went slick, shifting over the grip of my sword as the sun's first rays flashed across the horizon.

"He's here," a voice echoed from behind me, and I spun, my sword meeting the slip of cloth covering a high fey's delicate pink skin. The silk fell, and the fey's tongue darted out, tasting the air. It was a changeling named Liana, and although she'd spent a fair share of her time in the elven lands, I could not fathom why she'd risked appearing in the castle in that particular moment. Her flesh flickered briefly before the color blended into the same cool steel-gray of my sword.

5

"What are you doing here?" I asked levelly.

Her mouth twisted into a cunning smile. "Protecting my investments."

The chatter rose behind me, and I knew we didn't have much time. Liana blinked. "What do you want?" I asked.

She nodded, clearly pleased by my willingness to listen. I could feel the weight of Grey behind me, protecting my back from the other fey. Though the morning air was cool, their fires had made the overfilled room stifling. Liana ran a clawed finger over her bare middle, exposed by the cut of my sword. "It is a trap," she offered. "Do not spill the blood of the high fey."

"How is it baited?" I asked.

Her eyes rose to the ceiling as if I always asked the wrong questions.

I gritted my teeth. "Why do they bait me?"

Her gaze hit mine again, the firelight flickering against an otherworldly black, like a newborn kitten… One who might swallow a grown person whole. "There," she said, "lies your answer."

There was a sudden change in the pitch of the tension beyond us, and Liana's head cocked to the side, the movement too swift. Her slender ears tipped toward the corridor. "You are in need of my assistance. I shall return to you soon."

She dropped the tattered silks covering her, her silvery flesh darkening to the color of stone. She was gone from the hall in an instant, but she'd given me a warning, and the fey didn't offer them twice. I glanced over my shoulder, the golden glow of the fey god's wings already in view. He'd not come alone. Seven and twenty dark-winged shadow stalkers lined the broken wall of the eastern hall. The flame boiled down to nothing, thin trails of smoke dissipating to reveal the blackened stone. Flora and Virtue were not among Veil's court, and I wondered what task could have been more important than visiting the elven high lord.

I straightened, sheathing my sword to turn to the crowd. Veil's eyes were pinched at the corners, and I was sure he was trying to sense who'd been there only moments before. I showed him my teeth.

He straightened, coming to his full height as his feet touched the ground, and I was grateful, at least, that I did not have to witness his usual display. He flicked one of his wings.

"What is your purpose here?" I gestured toward the army of high fey at his back. "Our custom is to kill those who break in uninvited."

He ran a hand across the bronzed skin of his long, muscled abdomen. I did not let my eyes follow it. "My dearest Freya," he crooned, "why must you meet my calls with such venom and steel?"

The rising sun through the tips of his wings looked like glittering crystal, but his face was not so shaded that I couldn't see the warm amber of his eyes. I crossed my arms, all too aware of how easy it would be to blast him with an over-whelming surge of power. "You destroy my home and bring your legions, and then plead for hospitality?"

He stepped forward, and spoke in a low voice. "Be careful of your words, lovely, or I may show you what it is to truly beg."

My hand tightened on my sword hilt.

Veil smiled. He turned a palm upward genially, encom-passing the twenty-seven at his back. "Legions they are not, but I do let them handle a bit of the drudgery of late. I tire of the paltry collection of opponents." His head came down, and he watched me from beneath a lowered brow. "There are much more interesting challenges worthy of my time."

Some part of me wanted to curse him, to spit *I am bound.*

Chevelle was tied to me, not only through our power, but to our very cores. It was intimate, intrinsic to who we were, a bond that could not be broken. But pointing that out would only put Chevelle's life in danger and make him a target for any fey who wanted to win their lord's favor, and Veil knew that.

"My time is worth something as well," I said. "Now get on with your business and take your shields along when you go."

His jaw tightened with just a tiny shift in the muscle between it and his tall, narrow ear at the implication that he needed protection. I'd been so near that spot not so long ago and could still remember the scent of him, how he'd perched above me while my limbs lay numb, incapacitated by his poison. My muscles tensed at the memory, wanting to repay him the offense.

We stared at each other for a long moment.

Veil's shoulders relaxed as he turned to pace the room. After a length and a half across the smooth stone floor, the motion became a slow strut—he was returning to his usual mood. Grey shifted beside me, and I nearly jumped. It was so easy to forget everything else when Veil was in the room.

I cleared my throat.

Veil turned to me, his wings folding along his back as he placed a palm against his bare chest. "Forgive me, young Freya. Perhaps I should return when you are not so indisposed."

I leaned forward, curling my fingers into the grip of my sword once more. "I would think not."

"Well then," he said, "perhaps a bargain." He resumed his strut, the movement bringing him closer to where Grey and I stood.

"You know the old saying," I offered. "'Never trust a fey who still draws breath.'"

He tilted his head tilted toward me, his eyes gleaming with humor. His hand slid free of his chest. "Yes." He chuckled. "Most certainly true." He stepped nearer, and all shadows disappeared from his face. "But I was thinking more along the lines of a mutually beneficial arrangement."

"We have been at peace," I answered. "There is nothing I need to gain."

His mouth turned down in some imitation of sadness. I doubted Veil had ever known true grief. It wasn't in his nature to care about someone on a personal level. To him, people were prizes to be won. "You may not realize it now, but there is much you will need."

Liana's words echoed in my head. *You are in need of my assistance.* I hated not knowing. I hated their games. My voice turned to ice. "Is that a threat?"

He reached forward, running a finger across the pommel of my sword. "I would never harm you, my Freya. But there are those who would."

Do not spill the blood of the high fey. I swallowed hard, and Veil's eyes traced the movement down my throat. I felt bare, despite the long shirt and pants that I wore. I was going to have to start sleeping in my armor.

"Things have been set into motion," he whispered, "things that will disrupt the happy understanding between you and I."

"My *understanding* is that you and your kind are to stay beyond the boundary of the outer rivers. There is no call to be on our lands."

He lifted his finger from its place on my sword and flicked it mesmerizingly before my face. "Land is not a thing to be owned, dearest. We stay in the forests because it is where our blood calls us to roam."

"And our blood is here," I spat, "beneath this palace of stone."

He closed his eyes, obviously chagrined by the mention of the first fey war.

But I went on. "Your people threw off the balance, and the ancients struck the accord that allowed them to live."

His army of shadow stalkers waited motionlessly behind him, showing no hint of concern for what had occurred. The lesser fey watched in rapt attention, clasping their hands and quivering with pent delight. Veil sighed. "So long ago. And yet it still rings in my ears every time I cross to this barren land."

"Death cannot be undone."

He stared at me. "No, it cannot." His hand waited between us as if he might attempt to touch my skin, and I would have to decide whether to slice it free of his arm or risk the insult. But he didn't. Instead, he leaned closer, murmuring into the air beside my ear, "I could have won you once, collected your heart as well as your gifts." He pulled back so that his gaze could fall across my flesh and finished, "But now it seems I will have to wait until you yield." He straightened, flicking his wings out with a full sweep, his voice suddenly level. "You know where to find me."

Once Veil had cleared the broken wall, I glanced sidelong at Grey, who was sprinkled with golden shimmer.

"Charming," he said.

I laughed because we had an audience but couldn't decipher why the hall was still lined with the twenty-seven dark-winged guards. One of the winter sprites grinned.

"Grey," I said, "it's probably best we heed Liana's advice."

He nodded, but his foot slid outward as if preparing to fight.

We were the only two surprised when a scream echoed through the hall.

2

FREY

It wasn't a scream of pain as much as a cry of victory. It was that of an excruciating kind of success, when it felt as though death was closer than winning and it had taken everything to pull it off. It was a skin-of-one's teeth cry, one that meant the high fey had just claimed a significant prize.

Ruby, I thought, my chest clenching as I ran. I could feel Grey behind me, but it wasn't because I was faster than him—it was so he could protect us from the threat of the shadow stalkers we'd left behind.

Shouts rang through the corridor, leading me closer to some unknown disturbance. I tightened my hold on the power within me, knowing what it would cost if I made a mistake.

It wasn't Liana's warning I was worried about. It was that the fey could steal my strength, which I could barely control. Asher's death had gained me not only my crown, but a power too large to wield. In the time since, I'd wanted to secure our rule. I had insisted that Chevelle go on about his duties, but without him there to ground me, to stabilize and anchor the

11

overwhelming energy when I used it, there was no way to prevent one of the stronger fey—someone like Veil, who might be able to pull it from me for his own gain—trying just that.

Three water sprites rolled from a doorway and crashed headlong into the corridor's opposite wall. I drew my sword, prepared to dispatch anyone who tried to stop me, and felt the surge of frozen air behind us as Grey battled with a pair of frost monsters. Anvil stumbled from the room, head down as he thrust power into the small pale bodies of the fey sprawled across the floor. Blood dripped from Anvil's brow, and his leather breastplate was torn and hanging loosely from his massive frame. I shot past him, entering the room with Grey hard on my heels.

The library was chaos, with books, pages, precious scrolls, and ancient casting ledgers strewn across the wooden floor. I'd never seen that room molested by their madness, and the shock of it made me stumble to a standstill. They had lost all regard for it and had broken their own rules. They were a wild people, but they did have at least some barriers. If there was one thing the fey respected, it was knowledge.

Fire lit the stone before me, orange spikes of heat licking at my boots. There was ice behind me and the repetitive peal of Grey's blade. Smoke and the stench of sulfur filled the room, mingling with burned flesh, singed hair, and the sweetness of ripe summer fruit. Something sticky dripped from the ceiling to land on my arm, but I didn't look up. I didn't move. All I could see was Steed's prone form on the shattered bits of wood that had once been a mahogany table. A high fey stood before him, his liquid-gold eyes shining in challenge as they met mine.

I raised my hand to strike the fey, but my sword was still there, the heft of the metal all that kept me from the grandest fault: magic. I raised my blade, poised for a killing blow, and stalked toward him.

His wings were short and jagged, his muscled arms braced with fey steel that was not metal, but magic. It flexed with his movements and would slow a blade like the sap of a gum tree, but it was only covering his torso, and I wasn't aiming for that.

He hissed, and I swung. Magic shuddered through the air between us, but it was not mine. I could not let it go without an anchor, and I took the strike. As my blade came across the base of his neck, the power shoved me backward, and I only managed to slice the fey's wrist as I was knocked away. Tremors rocked my insides, the magic roiling through my chest cavity as it worked to tear me apart. I stared at the ceiling, willing the energy away, and the bronzed fey came once more into view. He stood over me, raising a hands to strike and whispering foreign-sounding words. My sword was lost to me—I could barely feel my hands. There was a short blade tucked into the quick-release scabbard at my hip, but I needed sensation to get it.

My power was screaming, wanting to tear free. I knew I could fight it. I could draw on that power and push his from within me. But if I left myself open, there was a chance I'd be releasing it to the fey. I had to keep it tied within me for the safety of the realm. When it came down to the end, it was better that I died.

I knew that kind of thinking was a terrible way to live and that I needed to focus on finding my reflexes before it got that far, so I closed my eyes, forcing myself to still. The air was hot around me, and blood dripped from the high fey's wrist to splatter the ground and my skin. The scabbard belt pressed into my back, the dagger's cross guard tight against my hip. It was made of cold, hard metal and was only inches away from the prickling heat of my palm.

With every ounce of my being, I gripped the dagger and thrust it into his thigh. He screamed, his energy crackling through the room, and I tried to make myself breathe. My teeth rattled, my ribcage felt as if it had been crumpled, and I wasn't sure my legs worked. I would risk falling. I clambered to my knees, but the fey grabbed me, jerking me up by my shirt to face him. One hand shifted to the skin of my neck, and his long, impossibly strong fingers tightened into what felt like a noose. His magic within me gathered there, boiling beneath his palm, ready to end me.

Over the fey's shoulder, I saw Grey step up behind him. I smiled. The fey opened his mouth to speak again, but I never heard his words. Grey was quick, and his knife went deep. We fell to the ground, the bulk of the fey hitting my outstretched legs as Grey was attacked from behind by a feathered fiend who'd somehow managed to get a club. My stomach dropped —it wasn't a club. It was a broken half of Rhys's staff.

I pushed the leaden weight off me, dragged my legs free, and drank in a painful breath. Grey dispatched the fiend quickly, but more and more attacked at every moment.

"Go," he said, and I did. The lesser fey weren't there to kill us. They were a planned distraction.

I got to my feet, and a lithe ochre form leapt at me, its bony hands searching for purchase, some bare spot of skin to make best use of its power. I punched at the thing's stomach, cracking bone, and then fell as my legs gave up what little strength they'd gained. That put me close enough to my sword, and as the beast clawed at me again, I cut it into pieces. I sucked in air, crawling clear of the chaos before I pushed to standing with the help of my blade. I felt suddenly disoriented, but in the fighting, I'd managed to make it to the opposite wall.

There was movement around me as Grey and Anvil and a handful of sentries fought the lesser fey that shot through the space, leaving pandemonium in their wake. I didn't see Rhys, but couldn't let myself think of that, or of anything, once Steed's full form came into view. He hadn't stirred in the slightest. One arm hung limply over shattered timber, its bloodied fingers empty of either motion or sword. Blood was caked on his hacked-up shirtsleeves, his leather armor shredded by claw and blade. I moved closer but was afraid to touch him, terrified of what I would find if I were to see his face.

I knelt beside him and placed a palm against the laces of his guard-issue breastplate, where they were already loosened by the cuts to his other side. My hand slipped beneath it, waiting for his chest to rise and fall. I kept waiting. My throat went thick, my eyes and heart hot with emotion, and then I choked on sudden hope when the smallest, weakest swell rose beneath my palm.

"Steed," I said with a deep breath, rushing to shift him onto his back. I lifted one side gently, forgetting somehow that I had the magic to elevate him. My skin was wet with blood— his blood—and I trembled and struggled until I could see his slack face. He was so pale, his features soft and unfamiliar. "Steed," I said again, certain that he was in there, firm in the knowledge that I needed him to reply. Some strange part of me wanted to smack his face, to wake him up from the nightmare.

I tore the breastplate free, slicing open what remained of his tattered shirt. The wounds had clearly bled freely, but the flow had turned into thick, slowly weeping red tears. I didn't know what to do for him or how to help. A terrible notion was clawed at me, saying it was too late.

I wouldn't let it be. I glanced over my shoulder, searching for anyone who might be able to help. *Ruby*, my mind kept saying. *Ruby can heal him*. But Ruby was gone. I could see none of the chaos in the room, only the long, thin gown of the now pink-skinned high fey. I was fairly certain she'd stolen the gown from one of Asher's old rooms, but I didn't care.

Liana stared down at me, her arms crossed over her slender chest. She tapped a finger where it touched her biceps. "I warned you, lordling."

"Help him," I said.

She flicked her hand, gesturing me aside, and folded her long body to kneel over him. "Go," she ordered, but she did not move to touch him. Her head tilted sideways, her eyes narrowed as she listened for something deep within.

"Is he—"

She cut me off with a snap of her fingers. I let my gaze trail down the side of Steed's still face, but I did not touch him, either. *This is not how I will remember him. He will stay alive.*

When I rose to leave, Liana spoke to me, her voice suddenly gentle. "Do not search for the halfling. Save the others. She will have her own path."

My chest tightened. I stared at her, hoping beyond hope that she could be trusted, and knew that I couldn't let any of what had happened keep me from what had to be done. I turned to face the room, but the fey were gone. They'd served their purpose.

Grey stood midway between me and the entrance, his face paling at the changeling's words. His hands were scratched and bloodied, his armor smeared with the glitter of so many of Veil's disciples.

"Where is Anvil?" I asked, and he pointed to the hallway. I

followed him out, both of us glancing at Steed and the fairy one last time, and found Anvil leaning against the damp stones of the corridor, panting heavily and stabbed with what appeared to be thin shards of glass.

"Ice fairy." He wheezed. "Devilish beasts."

I stooped beside him, my own body protesting as I drew the shards free. He winced but was too exhausted for much else. "I don't think they hit anything important," I offered.

"What happened?" Grey asked, each of us knowing he meant Ruby. *Where is Ruby?*

We watched Anvil and the pain that flickered across his face, which wasn't from his injuries. "It was a band of them. Spiders, I think. They must have been waiting on her." He coughed on a raspy breath. "She's a feisty one, though. Left a brute of a mess. I heard the commotion through the hallways and ran up here as fast as I could. She led them to the library. Must have thought they'd spare this room. It didn't work. I caught the tail end of it, the noise and light, and then they were gone. I stood here, aiming to picture which way they could have gone, when the fiends ascended. Swarm of them." He gestured toward the library. "That's about when Steed and Rhys showed up, but it was too late for much of anything by then."

"Where's Rhys?" I asked him, tucking his armor back into place. I tightened the laces to help staunch the bleeding until someone could stitch him up.

"Tracking." His sword scraped against the stone floor as he pushed unsteadily to his feet. "He and the wolves."

My heart quickened, and I thanked whatever fortune had sent me the ancients who lived inside their silver fur. They must have been there with Ruby or had picked up on some sign of the spiders' approach.

Anvil gestured down the corridor toward Ruby's suites.

"She'd set protections on her room, so there are a few bits of corpses, if you'd like to take a look."

"In a moment," I answered. "I have a decent assumption that there are twenty-seven of Veil's armed shadow stalkers still lining our east hall."

"Waiting for your response," Grey murmured. His voice was subdued, and I knew he was in a worse state than I at Ruby's disappearance and Steed's current condition. I needed to give him a task, one that would keep him in line. It was why I'd kept him at my side earlier instead of Rhys. I didn't stop to imagine what would have happened to him if he'd been in the other's place.

"Ride toward Camber," I told Grey. "Find Chevelle and let Rider know. Anvil will stay with me until the rest gets sorted out."

"I don't think that will be necessary," Anvil put in. When my gaze cut to his, he explained, "Chevelle set two hidden sentries outside the castle walls. At the first sign of trouble, they were to report to him in town."

He'd concealed guards to watch us. Things had been at peace, and yet Chevelle had been waiting for something to happen. Even though he was my Second, he was still head of the guard.

And Ruby... Ruby had set protections in her own suite of rooms.

I was the only one who'd felt safe in the castle. I was the only one who'd let down my guard.

"Right, then," I said. "Come with me."

3

FREY

WE ENTERED THE EAST HALL TO FIND THE TWENTY-SEVEN HIGH fey waiting. Given the height of the sun behind them and Anvil's revelation, I was fairly certain that Chevelle wouldn't be far behind. I scanned the row of shadow stalkers, searching for one who might be in charge.

They didn't appear to have a leader. I gestured toward the closest one when he centered the line. "You await a message for your master?" The fey hated that word. Veil might have been powerful and might have upheld their law, but he was no one's master. Despite the slander, none of the fey batted an eye. They had come expecting to be insulted, I was certain. "I have it," I said.

The fey I'd singled out moved forward, his dark wings and shadowed skin appearing strange in the brightness of the room. They were the fey Veil used to conduct missions in the nighttime, not parade in the light of day. That was what his heliotropes were for, his court made of a spectrum of deadly powers. They hung around his neck like the rainbow tassels of Grand Council had, boasting of what they could do.

But that threat was gone. Grand Council had fallen at the hands of my Seven and the people of the north. I wouldn't be cowed by fey on our own land.

The shadow stalker settled on the ground before me, towering and well-muscled and likely to overpower me if not for my sword. He was half again my size, and that would unquestionably be the outcome without my magic, but I only needed to stall long enough to think of a response worthy of the fey lord that didn't involve the death of one of his high court. It was too late to avoid killing a high fey altogether—we'd already dispatched the fire-winged beast that had wounded Steed. In truth, I had a strong desire to wipe all of them out.

"The treaty has been broken if one of my Seven dies," I said. He didn't seem surprised when I added, "The guard in the library is close, but I will wait for that vengeance."

The rush of boots on stone echoed through the corridor, and my decision came more easily. I might not have relished the task, but it had to be done. Boundaries had to be kept. Rules the ancients had set could not be broken.

Anvil stayed in his position, but Grey shifted beside me as if marking Chevelle's place.

"As for the one who was stolen"—I glanced down the line, wanting each of them to meet my eyes—"your kind has taken my left hand. Until she is returned, the price will be paid by each fey I can find." I leaned forward, hissing the last words. "And find them I will."

I felt Chevelle suddenly beside me, his palm brushing my back to let me know I had free rein. The fey would be an issue until I could garner my own control, until the power—too strong—could be contained by me alone. Until then, I needed Chevelle.

And I had him. I seized the shadow stalker's hand and

sliced it from his wrist. A chorus of screams rose through the hall, the rest of Veil's army trapped by my power and unable to fight while it was anchored through Chevelle. It was still volatile, too strong and terrifying to wield, so I moved through them quickly, personally taking the left hand from each. It had been an act of war, as Ruby was my highest guard, one of the Seven, and I could not let that kind of challenge go unanswered.

"Tell him," I ordered once the business was done. "Tell them all."

I shoved forward with the core of my power, pushing their bodies through the broken wall and beyond. A cloud of dark-winged figures, twenty-seven of the fey's best fighters, bounded and bobbled before their own power returned.

Veil must have led them to believe I would not use magic. I didn't know if that meant he was unaware of my bond to Chevelle, or if that too was part of his plan.

I'd been afraid their pride would have them returning and that there would be more blood spilled, but none seemed to have the inclination. Their shapes disappeared into the faraway haze of sky.

I turned to Chevelle. "Glad to have you back."

He didn't answer, his dark eyes filled with the heat of the attack. He'd been expecting something, but clearly not the loss of Ruby and Steed. There wasn't a speck of blood on him, and I realized I must look a mess.

"I'm not hurt," I said. "Grey has fared well, and Anvil took a few shots, but Steed is the only…" My words trailed off, unable to come up with an answer that didn't choke me. "Liana is with him now."

"Liana," Chevelle repeated, wariness flashing in his gaze.

I nodded. "She came before the others and offered a warning about not killing high fey."

"And did we?"

I sighed. "We did."

Anvil patted me on the back. "Not to fret. I got some of my own. As did Ruby, it appears."

"Spiders," Rider said.

Anvil nodded. "Did you see something?"

"No." Rider shrugged his quiver, which had apparently shifted during their rush from Camber, into place. "And only a few are capable of leaving no sign."

I felt my brow rise at his quick conclusion. Rider must have been studying the fey since the attack on the hall a few seasons before. "Well," I said, "I guess we'd better check her suites for some message or sign of her."

Chevelle touched my arm before I could turn to go. His clothes held the scent of the horses and the cool mountain air, a comforting contrast to the acrid smoke of the fire and fey. But he was too still, his broad shoulders too straight. With a guarded expression, he asked, "Did Liana give any other warnings?"

I bit my lip. "That we should not chase Ruby."

There was a stillness in each of us. I could practically feel the weight of Grey's stare. I couldn't make him choose between his oath to the guard and Ruby. It didn't matter because even I couldn't let it go unanswered. No matter what it took, I couldn't leave her to them. I could not abandon Ruby —she was a halfbreed among the worst of her kind.

Chevelle could see my decision, and we made our way through the maze of corridors toward Ruby's suites. It brought us past the library, and my feet faltered before I was able to look within. I stopped in the doorway, pressing my fingers to the bridge of my nose and biting back a growl.

"What is it?" Grey asked from behind me.

I shook my head. "She's gone."

The others glanced in, finding that Liana and Steed were nowhere to be seen. They moved on, probably expecting as much from one of the fey, no matter how long that particular one had been dancing across the borders to live among us. But Chevelle stayed.

I turned to him, and he finally looked up at me, his gaze leaving the bloody mess that covered the library floor.

It's fine, I told him with my eyes. *This is about Ruby. Ruby and Steed.*

We had been through much when I'd been taken to live under Council's watch, but this was different. I had been bound, unable to remember who I was or what I'd lost, and this was worse. Ruby would suffer. Ruby would know.

When we reached the hallway where her rooms were, it became apparent exactly how much fight Ruby had let loose. The stones were charred and covered in splatter, six different shades of tonic and blends. Ringlets of smoke still rose from the floor in patches, and the tapestries were in smoldering shreds.

There wasn't a sign of her attackers anywhere, aside from the few actual pieces of men. The spiders had a specialty in their ability to slide in and snare their prey as if indeed they were eight-legged creatures dropping from the ceiling on invisible threads. But these beasts did not have eight legs—they had two. And sticky as their snares might be, they had flown out of the castle, not unlike any other fey.

Anvil squatted beside some part, possibly a chunk of leg. "Doesn't appear she's lost her fight any. Must have been a bear to capture her. Likely they were ordered to keep her in one piece."

I couldn't imagine the struggle of anyone trying to take Ruby alive. I scanned the windowsills and doorways, searching for some hint of which way they'd gone. They would be impossible to trail. Once they'd cleared the castle walls, they would stay airborne until they reached the protection of the trees, and they were fast. The most likely path they'd taken was the northeast crag, flying low and out of sight to the first cover. "They're probably near Grenval's Peak by now."

We might have had a chance at finding her, maybe using the birds, but the fey had known as much. They'd known I could control animals and see out of their eyes from where I stood, directing them to action. I would have been able to track the culprits from the sky and attack them with every beast in range, but they'd hung around long enough to prevent anything of the sort. I hoped Rhys had found her. I prayed he was staying back far enough to keep himself from harm.

Grey stood in the doorway, his face pale, his hair disheveled. He couldn't seem to decide where to look.

There was no single mark in the entire space that didn't scream of the battle that had taken place there or of Ruby, fighting for her life against a pack of formidable beasts, being overtaken. Being stolen from her own home.

I straightened, my spine abruptly rigid with the anger of what they'd done. I wasn't sure why it had taken so long to affect me, for the full emotion of it to sink in. I'd done my duty and had shown my political response. But it had become personal. They'd snuck into my castle and stolen one of my guard from her own room. They were going to pay, and not just with a single hand apiece. "Grey," I snapped.

He looked at me, wrenched from whatever horrible scenario his mind had been playing.

I shifted the sword at my hip. "Ready the horses."

He didn't smile, but his posture eased, some part of him desperate to act despite all the reasons not to.

My eyes met Chevelle's, both of us knowing we were on

dangerous ground. Fighting the fey was one thing, but following them onto their land was wholly another—not to mention the warning against it.

Still, I couldn't do nothing. "Rider, gather what you'll need to track your brother." A list was populating in my head with all of the things we would have to do and all of the traps the fey would set. And Steed—*where had Liana taken Steed?* I pressed my eyes closed. "Can we please send someone to find that cursed fairy?"

"I'll put a sentry on it," Rider answered as he prepared to go.

"Thank you." I nodded, wishing that I could promise the safe return of Rhys—not simply Rider's brother but his only living family—but at that point, I didn't have such confidence, not if he'd followed them into the heart of the fey lands. *Had they reached the rivers by now? Would they be that far?*

My scrutiny returned to the walls of Ruby's room. I was certain she would find a way to leave at least some clue if she'd had any idea who was behind the attack, where they might be taking her, or why. Overturned bottles and broken glass lined her once-tidy shelves, the contents of so many elixirs trailing in dark streaks down the carved stone and pooling at the floor. The room stank of smoke, sulfur, and some earthy, unidentifiable residue. It was laced with a floral scent—almost untraceable but possibly amaranth and camellia oil. It was confusing, the jumble of so many of Ruby's spilled concoctions and the lingering sense of fey, so I left it to Chevelle and Anvil while I searched for something left out of place visually. It was difficult when everything felt out of place.

Once we'd exhausted our search, each of us ill from the fumes and filthy with tinted dust and the black smudges of burned cloth and wood, we headed to find Grey. We were

25

near Rider's rooms when I noticed that Anvil's wound had soaked through his shirt. He looked a little pale.

"Why don't you take a minute?" I said. "We'll gather Grey and Rider and meet you in your study."

His brow tilted, but he didn't argue. It was going to be a long ride, after all.

"And I'll see if I can't find someone who's good with a needle."

"Aye," he answered. "Someone decent enough."

Anvil moved more slowly as Chevelle and I continued, and I knew he'd fought the fey with everything he had. I wondered which of the high fey he'd taken. I hadn't thought to ask. In the scope of things, it hadn't seemed to matter.

We met Grey in the stables, where the horses appeared to be unharmed from the attack on the castle. He already had them saddled and packed, and Rider stood by his side. "We have a few things to take care of first," I explained. "It shouldn't be more than…" I glanced at the sky, surprised at the height of the sun. It seemed like days had passed, but I'd only been woken before dawn, and everything had happened so fast. "We'll be mounted by midday," I assured him.

They stood in the shadows of an overhang, and once we'd been there for a moment, I realized why. News had traveled through the castle, and we were starting to garner an audience, all waiting to see my response to the first official incident since I'd settled firmly into my role as head of the North.

I glanced at the palace staff—so many men and women depended on us, wagering with their lives.

It had happened too quickly. I had never wanted to rule or take Asher's place. I'd only wanted to get away from him, to save myself and the people I cared about. He'd left me no choice. It had been him or me. I would have endured years of suffering and betrayal at his side, the torture of everyone I loved, and the misuse of my power.

Chevelle's sentries were gathered in the courtyard with one of the castle's most proficient sentinels at their head. With dark hair cropped close to his head, a square jaw, and sharp eyes, Edan stood watchfully before the new recruits, undoubtedly hesitant to show them the lay of the land until this mess got sorted out.

"I should probably deal with this," Chevelle said with a note of frustration in his voice. It was perhaps the worst time to have brought in new recruits.

A tall girl in a dark tunic and pants caught sight of Grey, apparent recognition lighting her eyes. But her smile fell before it had a chance to take hold, likely owing to his expression. I wasn't sure he even noticed her among the crowd.

There were half a dozen of them, with fresh young faces from Camber and the surrounding camps. A stout male standing particularly still caught my attention, and I realized it was Camren's son. The boy had lost his parents to our cause, his mother Camren had died bravely in the battle against Council, and his father as a castle sentry. The boy's stillness made sense, as my own sight of him brought back those memories in a rush. I acknowledged him with a small nod, and he seemed to relax.

Chevelle exchanged a few short reports with the head sentry and gave him instructions for our upcoming absence. It reminded me of the scrape we'd been in, and I looked down, surprised again at my state. We probably shouldn't have been traipsing across the countryside looking as if we'd just slaughtered an army.

"I suppose we should clean up," I said, "though I doubt anyone's not heard of the scuffle by now." I turned to Edan. "If you've got someone skilled at stitching, Anvil could use a hand."

The girl in the tunic spoke up then, stepping forward only half a pace. "I can do it," she offered, her words directed not at me but at her next in command. Edan looked as if he planned to deny her, and she said, "I've got ten years of experience stitching the animals and no less than that doctoring those wretched rogues."

Edan's lip twitched, possibly because Anvil would not normally have been lumped in with either livestock or rogues, but the man still jerked his head to silence her. She stepped back into her place, her gaze downcast but her shoulders straight.

Her dark clothing was worn and frayed, the leather belt tightened around her slender waist rubbed and nicked. I assumed the latter was from working with the animals kept outside of Camber, which provided the town's staple supply of meat. She looked sturdy enough to wield a sword, but I wondered what had inspired her to join the castle guard.

Grey had apparently come out of his contemplations and recognized the girl. He looked hard at Edan. "I can vouch for her. I've seen her work, and it's good enough for Anvil."

I had a feeling that "good enough for Anvil" meant that it was going to hurt and not necessarily look clean. But we were shorthanded, and not a lot of us had taken the time to learn how to close wounds properly. We'd had people to do that for us—people like Ruby.

"He's in the study," I told Grey. "Make it swift."

4

FREY

I RINSED MY SKIN CLEAN IN THE BASIN, THE WATER A GLISTENING pool of blood and ash. It took another pitcher for my arms and one more on top of that just to make sure I was truly clean. My thoughts kept returning to Steed's broken body, to Ruby's destroyed room, and to Grey's face as he waited with the horses, stroking them in steady, even movements.

"Slow" and "gentle" were not words I would normally have associated with Grey, but he'd been raised with horses. They calmed him in an abstract, absent kind of way. It wasn't like Steed's connection to the animals, which was as if they consumed his entire being. I could almost hear Steed's low words, his calming hum. I realized suddenly that a younger Steed must have shared those words with his sister, for they were the same soothing tunes Ruby had used to sing me to sleep so many times when my mind had been a mess of bindings and chaos.

All of that seemed so far away. I'd been rescued, restored to my home, and placed upon the throne, and Ruby was one of my high guard. It was easy to forget that she was a halfbreed like I was. She was different than me, though, because while I was half human, the part of her that wasn't elven was something stronger, something stranger. She was part fire fairy.

Ruby had the magic, and she was aware of the spells and trickeries of the fey, but she was also of our world. She had *lived* as an elf, despite the fire in her blood.

Given the feys' fascination with horses, it didn't seem a coincidence that her full-blooded mother would have found Steed's father, who bred the animals, for her own plot. But I didn't know much of the woman aside from that. She'd been desirous of power, and though that wasn't unusual among her kind, she'd gone above and beyond to get it. She'd researched, she'd planned, and she'd played deceit and wile at the level of fey legends. Most of them didn't possess that kind of patience.

Ruby had been her mother's prize for combining her magic with Steed's father's. What she hadn't known was that her prize came with a price. Her baby daughter had been venomous. It had cost her life.

So powerful. Deadly poison. A hand touched the small of my back through the thin material of my shirt, and I jumped, the clasp of my vest clattering into the bowl, where it settled against the bottom. The crest of my line stared back at me from the carved ornament as if a watchful hawk. The snake in its beak seemed to writhe beneath the rippling water.

Chevelle's arms wound around my waist, and I leaned into him. His chest was bare, his skin clean and dry.

But he hadn't been covered in blood, I reminded myself.

We'd had three seasons of peace, three seasons without bloodshed and the endless fear. Chevelle had made up for it. He had spent every spare moment simply *being*. I knew the seasons before had been hard, even once he'd found me and had managed to slip me away from Council's watch. We had been separated by a terrible chain of events, and I'd not been myself then—I couldn't have been trusted not to break. But he'd still been bound to me, regardless of the castings Council and Asher had laid upon me.

Chevelle had been bound to me, even when he'd had to use the long string of binding words that had never been my name and even when he'd had to pretend.

So many times, he'd wanted to touch me. I could see it now and understand, but he had been restraining those impulses. And he didn't want to talk about it, didn't like to think of the way things were before I'd been released.

It was over. I was his.

The bonds had been broken. Asher was gone. Fannie was gone. There was nothing hanging over our heads. I was finally free, or as free as anyone bound by the obligations of a crown.

I thought briefly of warning Junnie of our new trouble with the fey, but I was certain she'd already heard of the attack. She'd had a lot bigger mess than I'd come back to after our encounter with Asher's own half-fey child. At least my lands had some semblance of order—Junnie's entire system was new, given that the previous Council had been destroyed, along with a half-dozen of the northernmost villages and several trusted allies. She'd had to fight to keep the footing she'd gained and had used a harsh hand against those who'd opposed the change and what she'd done to initiate it.

Those things had been far from my mind recently, and when I recalled the idea of the small human babe in Junnie's care, I pushed them all away. I turned to Chevelle. "Who's doing this?"

He brushed a damp strand of hair from my face, his fingers trailing to the skin of my neck. "I don't know."

The truce between Junnie and me—between the kingdom of the North and the villages and grasslands of the South—

had been keeping a war at bay. The fey had no reason to come to us. The balance of power was intact.

"It's not about her, right?" Maybe it wasn't truly because they wanted Ruby.

Chevelle shook his head, indicating that he didn't have any more idea than I did.

"It can't be," I said. "They can't have started a war for one half-fey girl."

Neither of us mentioned the one that had nearly started over a half-human one. My mother had gone mad fighting Asher and inciting a battle between Council and the North that turned not just to bloodshed, but an outright massacre. We, any one of us, were fortunate to be alive, and me especially—I'd only made it through by a tenuous agreement between Junnie and Chevelle, by his maneuverings and the courage of my Seven. We had fought so hard to stay alive, and life was what we had in the present. It was all that mattered.

"It's not war," Chevelle said. "Not yet."

It would be, though, and I knew it. The moment we left, the moment we went after her, the fey would be waiting, and we would not back down. But it didn't matter. They would go to war over nothing. We'd seen it in the past.

"It got them riled up," I said, sliding closer into Chevelle's embrace. "The taste of it, so close. Just like the attack on Camber, they couldn't wait."

"If that were true," he offered, with one hand slipping lower to brace my hip against his, "they would never have bothered with the pretense. Not if enough of them were decided."

I sighed. He was right. We wouldn't guess, not with the fey. We would have to go, find Ruby, and discover what ridiculous web of trickeries it would lead us through.

I turned, leaving the clasp inside the basin, and Chevelle

took my hand in his. His hands were strong, so much stronger than mine, but it belied the gentleness in them, the warmth and tender attention that came every single time he wound his fingers through my own. He didn't speak, but the gesture said everything I needed to hear: *You have me. No matter what end.*

I nodded, pulling free to tighten my leather vest. Chevelle watched me, and I had the sense he wanted to offer to go in my stead. But he wouldn't.

Ruby was one of the Seven. It was my place.

I gathered my armor, lacing the long wrist cuffs on each arm. I wore all I could with metal plate, which was not a favorite of the fey. Sharp edges covered every part of me, mirroring the change in my mood. It was a prickling anger, hardened by the fact that I had no other choice.

Chevelle laced up his own shirt, drawing a leather breast-plate over his chest. It was centered with a carved medallion, the wings of the hawk curling beyond its edge. He wore the gear of a warrior as if he had been born for it, despite my own memory of the little girl who had never wanted him to be a soldier for the throne. We weren't children anymore, though, and it wasn't my grandfather's throne anymore. I was the only one who could do what had to be done, and I wanted Chevelle at my side.

"I'm going to head to the armory," he said. "I will meet you in the study when I'm done."

I nodded, knowing he would not collect simply blades. The armory held other weapons, including packets of dust and mixes, concoctions to fight the fey where our magic couldn't. There would be scrolls and spells.

And then Chevelle would be back at my side. It was the only way we could anchor my power.

I had a sudden, sickening surety of what we were about to risk. But I couldn't *not* go after Ruby—I could do nothing but give my life for any of my guard after what they had risked for me. The real danger was not my own life. The dread came because what was at stake was the possibility of Asher's magic falling into the hands of the fey.

Veil hadn't wanted it before, at least not so intensely. He might have had an interest in me, but the draw had little to do with this power. Until Asher, there was no magic that had the ability to break a realm, not on its own.

The nature of the magic in the light and dark elves was different. I remembered one of the rogue bands from when I was young—they'd scribbled their war motto across bloodied shields: *They grow, we burn*. It had been a taunt, but it went deeper than that. The magic wasn't interchangeable.

Except I had the blood of both, and I could harness it by default. I shook off the thought, seating my sword firmly in its scabbard as I walked toward the door. That was when I saw the pendant.

5

FREY

RUBY HAD KNOWN—MAYBE NOT THAT THEY WERE COMING, AND maybe not that she would be taken, but something. She'd left us a clue.

I clutched the pendant in my hand with no idea what to do. It had to mean something, to contain some message that only I could decipher. I glanced through the room once more, wondering when she could have placed it there. I had been sleeping when the guards had called, but by then, she must have already been contending with the fey. Something else had to have happened. Some hint had tipped her off, and whatever that thing had been was what Steed had tried to convey to me with his eyes, but I didn't know what it meant. He'd not known she was missing then, either. I'd sent them to find her out of my own fear.

The pendant had been a token passed to my mother when she'd become Asher's Second, his heir. She had given it to me out of spite. I'd only worn the thing when I'd been bound from using magic and the memory of what it had stood for had gone.

The metal clasp cut into my palm, sending heat and pain through my fist. *We have to put this all to rest. It should not still be the cause of so much distress.*

Chevelle had left the door open, so Rider caught me standing before the high table, and I knew my expression gave away my unease. "What is it?" he asked.

I glanced at him sidelong, letting the chain slip through my fingers as I worked to decide what to do. "My mother's pendant."

Rider stepped closer, his voice quieting. "The one that was merely a symbol?"

"Yes." I turned to him. "It's all that was left once she burned in the fire."

The fire should have ended the massacre. The fire had only ended her. The stone was all that was left of it. The chain that laced through my fingers was a replacement, the leather having been destroyed after I'd snapped it free of my neck the day Veil had placed a clue there. His clue had been a warning against Asher's half-breed children, who might ascend the throne. We'd figured it out too late.

I stared up at Rider. "What happened before Ruby was taken?"

He shook his head. "I wasn't there. Anvil said the others were playing in the study, an apparently affable game of chits. There was an argument, and things got heated. Rhys was posted on the far corridor, so he would have heard when Ruby stormed down the hall, evidently in a bit of a fit." His eyes narrowed. "She wouldn't have made it past the stairwell when Grey started after her. Anvil said he stopped Grey, warning him with some poor metaphor about knocking over a boiling pot." Rider almost smiled, but then his face lost all trace of humor. "Grey reportedly returned to the study, cutting off

Steed's attempt at conversation. It was silent for the next quarter hour or so."

"And that was when the guards called?"

He stared at me. "No. That was when they heard the wolves."

They had been spiders, and the guards had probably never seen them coming.

"She knew," I said. "She knew, and she left me this message."

"Rhys will find her. Whatever that means, whatever happens to that end, they will be together." Rider's words were steady, and I knew he believed them with unwavering conviction.

I slid the pendant into the belt at my waist. He was right, but I would do whatever I could to help them so that being together wasn't all they had. I walked past Rider on my way to the door, thanking him with a slight nod.

"Ruby is clever," he added. "But that doesn't mean her motives went unnoticed." Rider spoke to my back, but I didn't need to see him to understand the comment. Grey cared about Ruby in a way that kept his eyes from straying too long from her form and his mind preoccupied with her safety and well-being. He would have noticed something—something that might have had them bickering for longer than I cared to admit. Something had happened when I'd been bound.

My feet turned automatically, heading to Anvil's study to find the one person who could give us a better chance.

The girl was done stitching up Anvil's wound when we found them. Grey stood beside her, both of them tall and narrow. His words were low and the girl's face pale with concern. Her eyes met mine when Rider and I entered, and then she inclined her head and excused herself from the room.

"Grey, a word." My command was more clipped than I

intended. Something about the idea of him sharing Steed's condition chilled me.

He nodded, giving me his full attention without a hint of concern for what he'd apparently just done. But of course he wouldn't. Plainly, the girl had known Grey well, which meant she knew Steed. They'd likely all grown up together in Camber, before I'd even known Steed or Grey existed. And she was a healer.

We should be taking all the help we could get, I reminded myself. "There's something you're not telling me. Something about Ruby."

Grey's eyes never left mine. He never so much as flinched. But he didn't speak a word.

I stepped forward.

Grey's gaze didn't follow but stayed on the spot I had been.

"Do I need to rephrase that?" I did not make a habit of issuing orders to my guards outside of their normal duties or of using a strong hand, but I didn't like being kept in the dark. I would order him to break Ruby's trust if he made me.

His jaw shifted, his fingers twitching against a leg. "Whatever dealings Ruby had with the fey were kept from me."

"That doesn't sound like a denial." I reached for the pendant at my waist. "Why would you hide information when Ruby herself meant to leave me a clue?"

He jerked to look at me, clearly unaware of the possibility. I held my fist high, allowing the pendant to fall on its chain before his face.

"When…"

"I don't know," I answered. "I found it just now with my armor." I let my words sink in. "A gift with a connection to the fey, hidden among my battle gear."

"I—" Grey stopped, his mouth slack.

"If there is something you'd like to add," I said, "now would be the time."

Anvil cleared his throat, moving to stand. I didn't relieve Grey of my stare.

"Go," a voice said from behind me.

I turned, knowing it was Chevelle and hating the instinct that said I wasn't going to like what he was about to say. I couldn't remember the last time he'd cleared a room to give me news.

"We will be waiting at the stable," Anvil informed me. "Liana has been found, though the effectiveness of her treatments on Steed remains to be seen. Two sentries and Thea have gone to sit with him."

Thea, the new healer from Camber. I nodded, and the room was suddenly empty. I waited, watching Chevelle move toward me and feeling like the air was too thick to breathe.

"You know that difficult choices had to be made," Chevelle said.

I swallowed hard.

"There were very few options I could live with. Time was running out."

My stomach dropped. My knees locked, an old defense mechanism that had allowed me to stand at Asher's side, not letting on my surprise or hurt, hiding those weaknesses. It had kept me alive. "What did you do?" I asked.

"What I had to do." He stepped closer, not attempting to reach for me. He was a guard. He was my Second. He wasn't sorry. "What I would do again."

The pendant in my hand grew hot, my fingers tingling with power. It couldn't have been him. "Not you," I said, echoing the thought. "It wasn't you."

"To keep you alive," Chevelle answered. "I cannot regret that. Even if it means this danger to Ruby."

"You—" My words faltered, the idea so foreign I could barely process it. "You made a deal with the *fey?*"

His eyes were soft, but it wasn't regret for the deal, only the pain it was causing. "Why else would I have needed her?"

"That's… How could you? You know what they've done. You know how it goes. After everything—"

"I'm not going to apologize for bringing you back. No matter what happens, Ruby made her choices, and I made mine."

"She chose this? To be captured by the fey? I'm supposed to believe she's all right with what's happening to her… with whatever they are doing to her right now?"

"Of course she didn't choose this," he said. "Neither of us had any idea you would slay Asher or that the fey would take offense to this new power." He gestured toward me, making me abruptly aware of the heat emanating from my person.

I shook it off. "All of this has been happening behind my back. Were you even going to tell me?"

"It was safer this way."

I narrowed my gaze on him, but he made it clear he had no intention of backing down. "It was not your bargain."

The words cut me, and I knew he'd bartered too much. "What did you promise them? What prize do the fey think they have coming?"

He didn't answer, only stood stern and severe, the head of my guard. I dropped to a seat, my pendant-fisted hand pressing into the wood bench to keep me upright. "They will take her, and they will take you, and all of this will have been for nothing."

Chevelle stepped forward, placing a hand on my shoulder. "Ruby made her own bargain. We were not party to the other's deals."

I stared up at him, loose strands of hair falling over my

face. Ruby should have braided it. Ruby's work would have stayed in place. "Is there any chance we can get her?"

"No," he answered. "She will have her own path."

My jaw went tight, and I was suddenly on my feet. Liana's words had just come out of the mouth of my second-in-command. "The changelings? You made a deal with the *changelings*?" For an instant, I had a flash of understanding for Asher and the snap verdicts and sharp punishments he had doled out. But I wasn't him. I would never be like him.

"I won't bring you into this," Chevelle said.

"You can't refuse," I shot back. "I'm not asking as your—" I pressed my eyes closed, searching for composure. I waited two deep breaths. "A deal made with my Second is *more than* my concern. We are nearly at war here, and I will not go into this blind."

Chevelle's expression remained unchanged.

I bit back a nasty curse. "Tell me you understand my position."

"This is the fey we're dealing with," he answered. "Anything I tell you can only make your position worse."

I cursed aloud because he was right. All that time, I'd been wondering how we'd gotten into the position we were in, but we'd never been out of it at all. It was still the same problem. It was still Asher and being trapped between bad and worse. The only thing different was that we'd exchanged Council for the fey.

I couldn't say it was an improvement.

"Let's go," I told Chevelle, the words bitter on my tongue as I walked from the study without another look back at him. I hated that he was right, but I hated more what he'd had to do for me.

I hated that I couldn't say I wouldn't have done the same.

WE FOUND ANVIL, Grey, and Rider at the stable, armored and ready for battle. Like Chevelle and me, they'd opted for metal, spikes, and long weapons that would allow them reach but ease of movement. Though the others didn't have to worry about their magic being stolen, it was always a risk to use it to fight the fey—it had a way of turning against us, and that said nothing of the perils of fighting an enemy who could fly. We were heading into dangerous territory, with the deadliest of opponents lying in wait.

"Mount," Chevelle ordered, and my guard—what was left of it—obeyed with an eagerness that belied our task.

We rode through the southern gate, switching back to follow the rocky path that headed into the grasslands between us and the fey forests. The boundary dividing the lands wasn't a wide swath of earth, but it was enough, an open field cut in half by exposed bedrock and flowing water. It was a border that did more than signify the change—it protected us. It had been built by the elves, specifically to interfere with the fey powers, eons before.

Once we passed that, however, we would be on our own. The sky was ominously devoid of birds, the land surrounding us still. They fey knew of my gift and how I could I could seek out animals to survey the land. They'd obviously planned ahead to stop me, and it wouldn't be the last ploy of theirs we encountered before the day was out.

6

THE CHANGELING

LIANA WRAPPED A FRESH POULTICE OVER THE SUMMIT BOY'S shoulder, though the motion was purely for show. The last draw she'd taken from his chest wound had come out clean— there was no tang of poison left in his blood. She pressed and wove, her fingers moving nimbly to interlace the gauze and plant bits across his skin, and tried not to look at the others in the room. She should have taken her patient elsewhere, but the prying eyes were not as dangerous as those of her own kind.

The elven girl moved closer and squinted at the way Liana's hands had slowed. Her palm traced the ridge of the boy's ribs beneath his skin. "I'm not going to *eat* him," Liana snapped, only to immediately regret her words.

The girl crossed her arms, the gesture bringing her closer, somehow. "I should imagine not."

One of the two sentries posted at the narrow room's entrance watched as well, her hair in a too-tight braid, her fingernails tapping against a shining metal blade at her hip. The entire situation set Liana's teeth on edge. A hundred years before, she would have slaughtered them all and been done with it.

"Perhaps if you'd give him some space," she said, "he could work the toxins out of his system."

The cock to the girl's brow said, *Wouldn't you like that?*

Liana rolled her palms upward, the sticky ochre goo sending its scent across the space. "No matter to me. It changes things not if one elven guard lives or dies." She let her gaze fall casually to the bedside bowls and bottles. "Enough of the high fey have been slain to even the balance."

"Oh, please," the elven girl answered. "I've known your kind long enough to know you'd never do *anything* for free." The girl turned away, muttering something that sounded like "out of the goodness of your own heart, my brown-haired lass," and Liana smiled at having a new idiom to use.

Liana quickly put her grimace back in place before anyone had seen. "You and your kind," she said with a sigh, "always naming a price for life and tasks." She didn't know why she was speaking. She couldn't seem to stop herself. The words cost her something, each of them spilling out of her with the magic only an experienced changeling could muster. The changelings couldn't speak naturally—the words had to be brought to life with dark magic. It used valuable energy and time, and it tasted horrible. She should have just killed that elven girl.

"Thea," the girl said.

Liana's dark gaze snapped up to look at her. She knew she'd not spelled the thought to life. She had not spoken aloud.

"If you're going to glare and plot behind those beady little eyes, you should at least know my name." The girl's hand was still, too still, and covered in a thin latticework of scars. She'd meant Liana should know her name before the girl had to kill her. Liana laughed, the sound a bark of magic and ire.

She was done wasting words on the foolish girl. She stepped forward, not even bothering to clean the mess off her hands. And then the sharp *plink* of metal hitting glass drew her up short. She turned toward the window, crossing the space to find that her pixie had somehow missed that the windowpanes were in place and had crashed onto the stone-crafted ledge.

Liana shook her head, moving to undo the carved wooden latch and swing one side open. She stared down at the pale-yellow form where it had fallen on the frame. The pixie sat up, dragging the metal link it was tied to—a punishment from the thing's last betrayal, badly battered and dinged from exactly this sort of event—up to stabilize its weight.

"The lordling," the pixie wheezed, pushing a wild nest of hair away from its face with the back of a filthy little hand. It stared up at Liana with those disconcerting daybreak-yellow eyes, panting for air, exhausted from flight.

"What?" Liana snapped.

The pixie gasped another breath. "She and the others," it said, "the lot of them have fallen into a trap."

7

FREY

It was the shadow stalkers. It had to be. No one else would have been able to leave such a large snare in place without some sign.

I was in a haze of darkness and pain, the worst of which seemed to be crushing my chest. Not one of us had seen it coming. As soon as I could move, I dragged a hand through the thick black mess that covered my face and was stealing my air and sight. It stank of tar and tree sap, and it clung too tightly, yanking my lashes and skin. Gasping and gulping at air that seared my lungs, I scrambled to right myself. I could feel Chevelle through my magic and knew he was close enough to anchor and fight whatever was out there, but I didn't want to reveal my hand too soon. I couldn't know what was coming next.

"Grey," I called.

"Here." The answer came from behind me, and from the sound of it he'd not been hit as badly.

My ears still rang from the impact, the side of my head throbbing from collision with the ground. At least I knew I was on the ground. I could feel the broken rock beneath me. "Anvil," I said next.

"Aye," he answered. "Here with Rider."

That was bad—it meant Rider couldn't answer. They all must have been thrown as well. I wondered what of our horses—captured by the fey and already spirited away, I presumed. My mind was running through scenarios, creating brutal images of an injured Rider. It was all happening so quickly, the space of a few heartbeats slowed in time.

How long had the fey had to move now? How much of an advantage did they gain with every struggled breath?

"Chevelle?" My voice had grown lower. I was aware of him but needed to hear he was well and to get a status update on our enemy.

"They are in the west trees," he answered, his reply even quieter than mine.

I cursed. "How many?"

"Might as well clean yourself up," he said. "It looks like we're going to be here a while."

I went to draw magic, but Chevelle's hand was on mine, pulling me to him and wiping whatever it was free. The cloth he used had its own scent, sharp and stinging. I couldn't tell if it was simply a cleaning agent or an antidote. "Poison?" I whispered.

He shook his head.

I could finally see, and I let my gaze fall on the tree line over his shoulder. A few hundred eyes glimmered back at me, waiting. "So they don't want us dead."

Anvil's even voice sent a chill down my spine. "Not yet."

8

THEA

"Why are you just standing there?" Thea barked. "Go tell Edan something has happened!"

The guards flinched, and Thea wished she could remember their names. The tall one, a stout woman with five-strand braids, reached for the door while the other stammered, "But Liana... she said we should stay."

Thea marched toward the man, her fists clenched at her sides. "And when did the high guard start taking orders from the fey?"

His gaze fell, and both guards took to a full run the moment the door was latched behind them.

Thea didn't know what the pixie had said, as couldn't understand the creature's strange tongue, but based on the thing's gestures, some of which she did recognize, it couldn't have been good. A trap. Danger. *Help*. Thea's stomach dropped, her skin tingling and hands alight with the need to do something. She was certain things had gone from bottom-rung bad to worse-as-worse-can-get. They were in the mud—she knew it—and the fey were the wrong creatures to try to wrestle out of it with.

She returned to Steed's side, running a damp cloth over the bruised skin of his neck and arm. The changeling woman had given them no further information but had merely flicked the pixie free of the sill and slammed the shutters back in place. "Bar the doors!" she'd ordered. "Let no man enter this room."

Is she going to help us? Does she truly aim to save an elven lord and her guard? Thea couldn't believe it, even with the work the woman had done to save Steed. Thea's fingers brushed his skin as she worked, and she couldn't help but wonder at the way Liana's had done the same. There had been too much tenderness in it and too much of something that reeked of possession.

"Cursed fairies," Thea muttered, dropping the cloth into a basin, where it splashed among the remaining roots and herbs.

"Cursed fairies," a voice agreed.

Thea jumped, a hand moving to her knife and breath seizing in her chest. Steed groaned.

She went to him and brushed a palm against his head and his chest, finding that his temperature and pulse seemed if not well, at least appropriate for the situation. His eyelids stirred but did not open. She flicked her wrist at the torches, knocking the fire in three of them out to dim the room.

"Hold there," she told him. "Let me help you." She dipped a new cloth in the basin, running it over the skin of his face. The fey woman had covered nearly all of him with paste and powders, though Thea was certain only of what a few of them did. "You're safe here," she promised. "All is well."

He breathed out slowly, the motion relaxed and grateful. Thea always had been a good liar.

"I can't move my limbs," Steed said.

"Yes," Thea answered. It was how all the healers dealt with serious injuries to horses and men—immobilize the victim. "We're patching up your arm is all. You've got a bit of a nasty one there."

His brow drew down, his face tensing in pain. "I don't remember," he said.

She brushed his face again, warm water trailing through her fingers to drip off her forearm and wrist. It splattered to the floor at her feet, echoing in the empty room. "It will come to you. You've been given a tonic to help with the pain, and it's probably slogging up the memory."

"Ruby," Steed murmured.

Thea didn't reply, not wanting to explain that the treatments had come from a changeling and his sister was nowhere in sight. Ruby had gone missing, the other recruits had said. Thea hadn't believed it at first, but then they were there, a handful of the renowned Seven and the half-human girl who'd become the ruler of the North. Thea had never seen Lord Freya before that day, but by the looks of her, it must have been a terrible battle. She'd been smeared with blood and fey tonics, with scrapes and scratches covering her skin. She'd not looked entirely defeated, but none of her personal guard had shown much in the way of hope. And she'd never seen a man with more taken out of him than Grey.

Her mouth turned down at the corners. "Are you having much pain then?" She pressed her fingers into Steed's palm, worried he was coming out of it too quickly and wanting to check for reflexes that shouldn't have been there yet.

"Where is—" His eyes tightened again, wincing as he worked to find a way to open them. "Was there a fire?"

"Tsss," she hissed. "No need to force your memory. Let it come."

The sound was one she'd used on the horses, but she real-

51

ized her mistake too late. Steed's muscles, the ones that had regained their strength, tensed. He managed to open one eye and peer at her.

She smiled. It seemed unfair, given he'd not the ability to jump or flinch from her, but she figured she probably owed him one. Her nose scrunched up involuntarily at the thought.

"Thea," he whispered. His gaze moved frantically through the room as though he was in danger and not just merely disoriented. "Where am I?"

"Not to worry," she promised. "All is well." She pressed a hand to his chest in an effort to still his urge to run or fight. "You are home, in your castle away from Camber." She leaned in. "I have come to visit you."

His mouth formed a small circle in his confusion.

She patted his chest. "It will come to you. All is well, I tell you. You are safe."

"Why do I not believe you?" he said.

She grinned, cocking a brow. She'd missed Steed. She'd missed all of them. "Remembering a lost bet or two, Mister Summit?" She shook her head. "Some boys, they never learn."

Thea might have been a good liar, but the Summit family had never been fools.

"Now," she said, pushing her hair back from her face. "Be still and quit your chatter. I've got some mixing to do."

It was the first true thing she'd said to him. If she didn't get a new tonic in him before Liana's wore off, she was going to be corralling a wounded bear. It might have been a while since she'd seen Steed, but she knew his character.

The moment he found out his sister was gone, nothing would stop him from going after her, injuries and all.

9

RUBY

"Vex you, heathen goats!" Ruby spat, jerking a shoulder despite the eight-way restraints holding her down. The ties at her wrists cut and burned, their magic some sick combination of spell-woven hemp and plateroot. "When I get free of this"— she let her narrowed gaze pick off her captors one by one —"I'm going to brand you like the fetid livestock you are."

She'd been cursing and sputtering since the last of the rock-strewn ridges, and she was nearly out of productive expletives. At that point, the exercise was wearing on even her, but it was the irritation of her captors that she was truly after.

None of them so much as looked at her. Finally.

She let her head drop back for one brief moment, centering herself for what was about to come. And then she spun—tethered to a spit as she was—binding the hands of the spider at her feet within his own woven rope. They'd not trusted her to be secured only to the rod, despite the fact that she'd never been able to fly, and it was about to be their undoing.

The cold metal pendant she'd finally worked free of her leather corset had slid on its chain up her exposed breastbone when she'd thrown her head back, and it dangled within reach —if only she had the unrestricted hands to seize it. She flipped again, bucking and jerking until it bounced off her chin, and then she was chasing it, twisting her neck while the seven remaining spiders struggled to regain control. Two of them jerked from opposite ends, and she was strung back to straightened, the force of it nearly making her cry out.

But she did not, because clasped within her teeth was the small golden pendant that had taken her half the day to work free. One of the spiders gave her a strong elbow to the back, and the spit she was tied upon rocked as they righted her once more.

"Still yourself, halfling, or we shall skin you on this pole and taste the meat off your bones by nightfall." The spider was tall and lean, with ebony tattoos adorning the curves of his face and the sharp lines of his eyes. He leaned in close. "Would you like that, halfling? To go in fire?"

Ruby smiled. It was not the nicest of smiles, tinged with a bit of malice and short on teeth. But she'd not much to work with, given the pendant perched between four of her front teeth. She chomped down, the warning call from the spider cut short as the powder reached his throat. His expression fell, the muscles of his face giving way an instant before those that helped him breathe. He clutched his chest, stopping despite their procession moving on, and another spider glanced back to see why he'd faltered.

Ruby closed her lips around the crushed pendant and blew. The remaining powder caught the spider sidelong, but it was already relaxing the blink of his eye. It would work.

She just had five left.

One spider's fist busted her in the jaw, throwing the empty

pendant to the ground. She spat, but none of the residue was left in her mouth—all she could taste was blood. They were being smart. They kept moving, marching deeper into the shadowed forest, nearer and nearer what she feared was the worst place she could end up, not stopping to drop her or kick her ribs again, which left her with a harder fight. She needed to get within reach of them. She needed to finish it.

"It's too late for you," she told them. "The poison is spreading. Do you feel that tickle in your throat, that itch beneath your fingers?" It was trickery, but she couldn't have been so far off. None of them had stopped for a drink since they'd left the castle, and she herself was feeling the strain of a long day's fight. "That's the first sign," she promised. "Soon, it will reach your blood. Soon, it will crawl into your heart."

She heard the tearing of cloth, some shred of fabric ripped from the spider's thin cloak, and a tattooed hand moved to muzzle her. She snatched at it, biting down hard, and worked not to gag as she clamped her teeth tightly against bone.

The spider screamed, burning-hot venom leaching through the wound. The caravan stopped then, the remaining spiders dropping the spit to free her current victim. The force of it was too strong for her damaged jaw, and he was pulled from her grasp as she slammed into the packed earth beneath them.

Packed earth. They were too close.

A thin leather boot slammed into her stomach, and she retched, blood and bile pooling into the dark green moss. The earth was damp and cold, and she pressed her cheek to it, willing her weak limbs to feel their fight once more. She could not let herself be taken there. She could not let it be the end.

The boot came at her again, shoving her contraption and all to stare at the canopy of trees. It would be getting dark soon, turning to black night in the kingdom of the fey. The spider cursed at her, his narrow face and long brow formed into a menacing scowl.

She could let them kill her here. That would be better, she supposed. "Curse you," she muttered back at him. "May the fires of Hollow Forest swallow your screams."

He kicked her again, letting go a drawn-out, nasty line of expletives regarding her mother and some supposed mating with horses.

And then his words cut off, choked in half. Ruby stared in shock, her eyes wide and mouth agape. The spider stood above her, his silken cloaks and woven leathers unmoving in the still air as the shaft of finely carved wood protruded from his chest. The wood was familiar, crafted by magic and turned deadlier by one simple trick.

She drew in a sharp, hysterical breath. It was a poisoned arrow.

The air whistled with two more shafts, and the spider before her fell to the ground at her feet.

She whispered her mental count of the captors at her side: "Four."

She was shoved in the scuffle that followed, but she'd spotted guard-issued boots in the instant before she was moved. She heard two more muffled thuds as spiders dropped to the ground and then the snuffling of breaths, the pad of paws. It was the wolves. One of her Seven had come with the wolves.

"The forest," Ruby called to them. "There are six and ten in the forest."

"Three, then," Rhys answered. "We took out thirteen in the Cold Pines."

Ruby breathed deeply, something like a sigh. She heard rustling then and thought it to be lesser fey watching as their trophy was carried to the keeper. Someone called out, and there was more shuffling around her, the heat of fire, a blast of wind, growling wolves, and the sound of tearing meat.

Then it was quiet, and Rhys was unlacing the ties at Ruby's hands and feet. Her arms felt weak and prickly, and she couldn't quite find the control to bring them to her sides or rub her wrists. *Salve*, she thought, *what I wouldn't give for some salve*. Had her feet been bare, she might have had worse wounds along her ankles. But she'd been lucky, at least that they'd taken her in the dead of night, and she'd been dressed for fighting. She'd been fortunate that she'd learned to plan ahead.

Rhys inspected her wounds swiftly, giving a cursory glance to the bruising that covered the side of her face. "On your feet, Ruby."

She stared at him, sudden horror stealing her calm. "Where are the others?"

"Anyone knows." He glanced over his shoulder at the wolves still on high alert.

"No." Ruby grabbed his arm, her grip pained and feeble, her fingers covered in scuffs and tonic and more than a little blood. "No," she told him. "You can't be here alone. There have to be more of you."

Rhys gave her a glance. "Take it as it is, Ruby. Now, I suggest you find your feet."

Run, she thought, *find your feet and run*. But it was too late for that, too late for even the words. A cloud of ash fell upon them, sudden and heartrending. All she could do was tighten her grip to give Rhys one final warning before the burning wind hit them hard. A wolf screeched, a terrible yowl that fell dead against the thick forest surrounding them.

"They're in the trees," she choked out. "They're taking us to Hollow Forest."

She felt Rhys flinch. And then there was nothing.

10

FREY

WE WERE CENTERED IN THE RAVINE WITH A SHALLOW CREEK
running over the rock behind us and open grass before the
line of trees. We'd made it through the water before they'd
gotten to us with some explosion of magic that I'd not quite
pieced together, given the pounding in my head.

I stood, biting down to ward off the pain that stabbed my
side. Chevelle and Grey had gotten to their feet as well, but
Anvil stayed kneeling beside Rider, pressing a palm firmly to
the space between his shoulder and chest. It ignited fury
in me.

"Out with you," I screamed.

Scattered giggles echoed through the trees, but the leaves
did not shiver. I blasted the thick trunks of a half-dozen,
blowing them from the rock-strewn earth below. Chevelle
reached for me, his touch a reminder of my mistake. I tied the
power through him, watching as the lesser fey scattered over
the ground and into the air. The sun was getting low in the
sky, bruising the clouds and glinting off of fey wings.

"This ends now," I warned, stepping forward and raising

my palms toward the broken line of trees. We had no time for the games of the lesser fey.

Eight dark figures crossed the space, and two more rolled out of the trees. A chill wind met my face, but the scent of the nature did not surround us. Grey stepped beside me, the quiet hiss of his sword passing metal the only sound. They were not simply lesser fey.

There were only three of us—four, if Anvil could find a way to leave Rider's side. I might have brought an army, but I hadn't wanted more. I hadn't wanted it to look like an act of battle and hadn't wanted to risk anyone outside my guard. The high fey would have burned through them in minutes in their own lands. With unrestricted access to the base magic, almost all of the fey were stronger there, too strong for anyone but the most powerful elves to fight.

It was why we'd never crossed into their lands without good reason. It was why Ruby was in such great danger alone.

"Come out or die like cowards," I told the trees. "This is your last chance."

A thousand fears swam through me. The fey were clever and treacherous, and we'd been caught. I knew there was more, some trap, some unseen plan they'd lain into place, and we were at risk of falling into it just by standing on the rocks.

I called the power forward. The earth beneath us shook, and stone rattled against stone. A line of high fey seemed to materialize in the clearing across from us, their gray forms shifting out of haze.

A curse slipped from Chevelle, who stood beside me. They were not the shadow stalkers we had expected. It was so much worse.

I drew my sword free of its scabbard, readying my stance for the coming blow. A low laugh rumbled through the ground beneath my feet, and the hazy forms slipped into clouds of smoke. Too quickly, the smoke was upon us, an ashen hand solidifying into a fist mere inches from my ribs. I swung, but my blade sliced naught but air, and a trail of smoke followed the steel. It curled and writhed, twisting again into a flesh-like mass, and then I was staring into the colorless face of a creature neither elf nor fey.

It was a spell—I knew it was a spell—but when the thing smiled, I couldn't help but take a swing again. "Who's doing this?" I asked Chevelle over my shoulder. "Who here has this kind of power?"

He was muttering words and gathering power—I knew he was forming a plan to stop them.

Grey answered for him. "There are too many of the spelled beasts here at once. If it's only a single fey doing this, then there can't be a handful capable, not at this level."

The most powerful fey rarely ran in packs, and these things looked too similar to have been created by different people. A vaporous form lunged, and Grey struck, his blade catching in viscous black goo. He jerked, brushing my shoulder with his, and added, "If it is merely one, this far out and near the boundary, there can be only one of two high fey behind it."

I knew the first possibility: Veil. But it wasn't his style. Even with the warnings, even with the fear of retribution from the court, Veil would never use such soulless abominations to do his work. That only left one other, and the idea of a dark fey who held no code but his own made my stomach turn. He was a man who would catch fire to any elf just to watch them burn. He'd been a plague, and I never understood why Asher had not dealt with the fool and been done with it years before. "Keane."

Chevelle stiffened beside me, but not, I thought, because he'd not already considered the possibility that Keane was responsible. His surprise was more likely due to the fact that I'd called the man out.

Black dripped from Grey's sword tip, melting rock where it landed before our feet. "You may want to hurry that up," Grey whispered at Chevelle, whose hands were occupied with both sword and powder.

The latter, I hoped, was something that might keep their insides from burning us alive.

My eyes fell again to the tree line, skirting those shapeless clouds that rolled in and out of form. He had to be out there. Keane had to be within casting range to make this work. The nearest mist went solid, and a hand reached for my throat. I thrust my blade forward into the thing's soft stomach and up through its head, but the action gained me no more than a spray of darkness as its remnants splashed against the earth before it hissed and sizzled, trying to eat up damp ground.

"Running water," Grey muttered from behind me. I scanned the field, wondering again how they'd managed to bring their magic so close to the elven barriers. *Had they poisoned it? Turned the Earth? Or had we been tricked, deceived into believing these were the same grounds?* No, not all of us. One or two, and they might have had a chance to disguise the area enough to deceive, but there were five of us, and none easily fooled.

It had to have been someone stronger, then, someone capable of a power that could overcome what lay beneath us.

"There," I whispered, finally seeing the source of the magic, but a mass of dark-gray flesh slammed into me, knocking me flat on the ground. There were six of them, suddenly formed and stable and shoving me into the dirt. Grey was moving, as was Chevelle, but I could see no more than flashes of them between the creatures that shoved at my head and neck. They were pushing me down, crushing my face into the damp clay. Their bony fingers covered my shoulders and limbs, clawing. I couldn't even feel for my sword beneath the weight of them.

It wouldn't help, I realized. I couldn't cut them. No one could cut them, not when their insides were poisonous sludge. There was a screeching howl, and something clamped onto the meat of my arm. I tried to scream, but my face was crushed, and when the burning started, I knew one had bitten through the skin. My body reacted, wanting to buck and fight, but there was no way to remove them. There were too many, and I was too small.

They weren't magic, so I couldn't even reach them with that. They were spells, darkness. They were words and power, vile and nasty and drawn from the earth, and no one could beat them without resorting to the same malevolence themselves. *Chevelle*, my brain told me. *Chevelle has the magic. He will save you. Just keep breathing.* I whimpered, the sound lost between the sodden clay and crush of hands. I was running out of air.

There was a blast of power, a percussion from the ground beneath me, and suddenly we were all flying through the air. I was weightless, being pulled in all directions, and felt the brush of many legs and hands. Some of them tried to grab me, grappling for skin and cloth wherever they might, but they were dissipating, falling into the mist from which they'd been formed.

I slammed into the ground on the other side of the ravine.

Chevelle had thrown me to safety, where the barrier of water and rock and ancient elven runes would keep more attacks at bay. My chest ached, my ears rang, and the bites from the spelled creatures continued to burn, but I was safe.

My temple felt damp, but it wasn't from the cold water trickling over stone. It was blood. My blood. Keane had spilled an elven lord's blood onto the ancient battle ground of the elves and fey, and I was going to have his head for it.

My fingers curled into the stones beneath me, finding clay and silt and the coolness of mountain water. I pressed myself up, fighting vertigo to stare across the field as the line of fey waited in their trees. Magic coursed through my hands, surging into the earth and shaking the stones. I sent it through the ravine and into the roots of those trees, crushing and burning and destroying as quickly as a breath. The tree line fell, age-old oaks and ashes and thorns crashing to the soil that surrounded them.

I was caught in a heartbeat. Sharply and quickly, snares wrapped around and through my magic, seizing it beneath the earth. Panic surged, and I tugged, instinctually pulling at the magic beneath me. It stayed there, caught in some net by the hundred fey. I gasped, the breath ragged and sharp. My skin was a thousand knives, and my chest drowned in terror. The true trap hadn't been the ravine at all. And it hadn't been the spells.

Those had been a diversion, a way to get me back across the barrier, to separate us—to sort me from my guard. Terror filled me, and my eyes shot to Chevelle as he stared back at me.

I might have thrown up my hands to warn him, but they were rooted to the earth, unable to release the magic and unable to draw it free. Something was coming, some new fey treachery, and hot, helpless tears threatened to break free. *Chevelle.*

Chevelle. I found myself mouthing the word, my one weakness and the one thing I was suddenly powerless to change. They had bested me. They had known.

"I'm sorry," I whispered.

Chevelle's brow drew down, allowing his confusion to

show uncharacteristically. And then he turned, threw his hands forward, and blasted power toward the fey who hid within the cover of fallen trees. They began to sway and grumble, moaning and chirping like a night forest, crawling knee over hand onto the downed trunks as they waited for what was to come—as they waited for Keane to reveal the rest of his plan.

11

VEIL

"Are you telling me it actually worked? The Lord of the North and her high guard fell for it?" Veil slammed a chalice onto their workspace, and Flora bared her teeth, hissing as weeks' worth of toil splashed free of its vessel.

Virtue smiled. "Like babes to a lodestone." She watched Veil while her fingertips trailed along the edge of the soft leather armor that protected her lavender skin.

Veil had a particular interest in the heliotropes, but it wasn't due to the hue of their flesh. It was that they could hypnotize, given the proper attention, and it was the one thing that could do him in. Because on the right occasions, it worked both ways, and they could gather bits and pieces of what others were thinking.

What Veil was thinking was bad.

You can't go to her, Virtue's smile seemed to say. *No matter what happens, you can't go.*

"Tell him the rest," Flora said from her place at the worktable. She'd not even looked up, but the power between the two was especially potent.

Virtue huffed, her fun spoiled. "The changeling had her own agents among those who laid the trap. She's abandoned her charge in the castle. It appears she heads for the elven lord with plans to intervene."

Veil felt his face go slack. "Liana?" She was an enigma in the worst way. It was impossible, but it seemed she consistently drew on the base magic whenever she needed it, no matter that the elven lands were barren and no matter that even he couldn't reach it among those lands.

"I will keep you apprised," Virtue promised, feral grin back in place.

Veil flicked a hand to shoo her away. It didn't matter anymore. Whatever the cost, it was too late to do anything but act.

FREY

KEANE STEPPED OUT OF THE TREES, HIS SKIN GLINTING IN THE sun like the husk of a sap beetle. He was huge, even from across the clearing, and his eyes were narrowed in a grin. "Caught!" he bellowed to his followers, raising his arms in a gesture that encompassed us all. "Netted in a web of your own making."

I growled.

Keane laughed. "Ah, but it is, precious Freya, for you have stepped onto fey lands." He sauntered forward carefully enough to suggest he was staying within two lines, as if he'd laid protection in advance. If that were true, we would not be able to retaliate with spells unless he was persuaded out of them. Keane's gaze roamed the field, purposefully finding my guard as he spoke to me. "We can forgive your trespass, I suppose, given that you are now on the other side. But your friends…"

His fingers curled inward, biting air, and I could feel the power building within them even from a distance.

Chevelle and the others were frozen, but I had no way of

knowing whether it was because of Keane's power or that they had nowhere to run. Electricity crackled in the sky, and heavy drops of rain splattered on only one side of the ravine. The trees were gone, but the wind rustled unseen through what still sounded like broken leaves. It was the worst of the fey.

I couldn't let my own power go, couldn't give it to Keane. I couldn't even risk walking across the barrier, not with it so firmly in fey hands and with the ravine separating us. And the others couldn't come to me, or it would look like backing down, and one never backed down in the face of a fey horde. My guard would be eaten alive by so many. And Rider was downed—I couldn't even see what was wrong with him because I hadn't had a moment to check. They wanted him, and they wanted Chevelle so that they had control of me.

I swallowed hard against a dry throat, with my ears still ringing and my pulse pounding at the wound in my head. The bites burned like hot coals, and it was spreading.

"I don't trespass," I heard myself say. "I come on invitation from your king."

Keane roared, moving forward and, apparently, nearly out of his path of safety. He checked his step, placing one foot firmly in front of the other. "We of fire have no king!"

I shrugged, the movement feeling like a dagger in my injured side. "King, chief, royal head of a demon court... I don't care what you call his gloriousness." I forced the corner of my mouth to twitch, despite the busted lip. "But he rates higher than you."

I scanned the clearing with my mind again, desperate for some sort of wildlife. A bird, a dog, a rabid muskrat... if it could just cross those magic barriers and get him off his feet, we might be okay. I wondered briefly if Chevelle would attempt to spellcast, but there were so many high fey surrounding us, and I was out of reach of all of them.

Keane shot a hand out, and fire blasted the ground at Grey's feet. Flame shot over Grey's pants like a lantern had burst, but it wasn't the heat of small flame. It was hot—boiling —and despite his familiarity with fire, a scream tore from Grey's throat.

Chevelle moved, apparently not frozen at the hands of the fey, and knocked Grey off his feet. The instinct to go to them pulled at me, but the power tied to the fey kept me in place. Chevelle was shouting and tossing powders and mixes from his belt, and I prayed Grey would be safe. I prayed for some way out.

I submit, my mind yelled. *Don't hurt them, let me submit.* But surrendering would do nothing with the fey. If they knew they had won, they would only toy with us further.

"You harm those of my Seven?" I challenged. "You dare raise a hand in aggression to those under the protection of invitation from the fey court?" I stepped forward, my boots splashing into the edge of moving water. "On this land created by the grace of the ancients who allowed you to live?"

Chevelle had put Grey's inferno out, leaving his leather pants intact but the sleeves of his shirt tattered and revealing blistered skin. Chevelle cut loose the metal armor, the heat of the fire turning it to a branding iron. If we got him out alive, and if we got Ruby back, she might be able to heal him.

Keane stared at me, no more bothered by the scene playing out before him than by the buzzing of flies. "Foolish girl, you think I don't know your threats are empty. What fey court would invite you unattended to cross our borders?"

"And yet you knew I was coming," I said flatly. *Because he took her? Because he has Ruby?*

He sighed. "These games grow old. I submit we move on to

new ones." His face was too narrow, his limbs too sharp. The shadows of those lines did nothing to conceal the spikes of bone, meant for tearing at flesh, destroying his prey. If ever a fey looked evil, it was Keane. He used it to his advantage. "There." He snapped his finger at the high fey to his right. "Have at them."

Liana's warning rang in my ears: *Do not spill the blood of the high fey.* It wasn't meant to caution me at the castle at all, I realized. *She meant here. The warning applies now.* Fey lands, the boundary, a truce and treaty created by the ancients… My chest thundered with a new thrill of fear.

I moved forward, the water's current pushing at my calves as I dragged the power with me, as two dozen high fey rushed Chevelle and Anvil, as Grey waited on his knees, and as Rider lay flat on his back. "Liana!" I screamed to them. "Liana!"

Chevelle's sword was drawn, his back to me as he prepared to fight, and I couldn't know if he had heard me over the squall of so many eager fey.

I braced myself, willing the words to cross the void, for him to understand the danger. "*Liana!*"

A soft splash sounded behind me, just light enough I shouldn't have heard it. But I had. "Yes, dear one."

I turned, my breath coming too fast, my chest sharp with pain.

It was Liana. She had come.

The clash of metal and boom of power sounded behind me, but the clearing was a mask of smoke and ash. Chevelle had conjured beast-things, narrow and viney, covered in thorns. *Or was that the fey? Trees spelled to life by the fire fey's horde?* I didn't know what was happening, but it was bad. A blade sliced through the clouds of smoke, and dark figures moved in and out. The lesser fey watched from their perches, hooting and howling despite the forest having been destroyed.

I couldn't see Anvil. I couldn't see Grey. I was going to let go of the power. I was going to go to them. I would walk away from my position and give up everything we'd tried to gain.

I wasn't strong enough.

Liana stepped beside me. "My," she said. "What a glorious mess we have here."

My gaze snapped to her once more, imploring that she fix it. She needed to do something before I ruined us all.

"A trade?" she offered.

"Liana," I growled.

She sighed. "Fine. You will repay me later."

Her lithe form moved forward, the pale pink of her flesh muddying as she crossed the river stones, momentarily going true-to-form until the water and smoke caught and shaded her to the steel color of a polished blade.

Her magic rolled through the clearing without much resistance, and I knew Keane had not yet joined the fray. He was letting his underlings play, giving them a treat for holding his line. Liana was strong. She was old for a changeling and had the years to gather magic and spells and the talent for collecting power into stones to use at her leisure. But Keane was stronger, and given the chance, he could break her in two.

When the smoke cleared, everyone paused, bloodied and breathless, the high fey grinning their pleasure as my guard stood beaten and bruised. Chevelle didn't look at me. He knew better.

"That one," Liana announced with a gesture toward Grey, "is a far bigger prize." Her voice rang clearly, the spelled words amplified, laced with magic not only to cut through the sound, but to truly be heard. "He is a toy of the halfling, and you'd be a fool to spoil him here."

Her head tilted, gaze turning to Anvil. "And he is more powerful with the elements than half these high fey." She clicked her tongue. "Honestly, Keane, you disappoint even me." She hadn't mentioned Rider, for which I was grateful. There was no sense in pointing out the one whose brother might be on the spiders' tails, the one person who had a chance of locating Ruby.

Keane straightened, the sneer wiped from his face. He didn't like Liana, but I wasn't sure he would kill her, not when she had ties to so many of his kind. Not when she'd made so many deals.

"Be gone with you," he answered. "This is no business of yours."

"Ah, but it is." She shot a finger toward Chevelle. "That one is mine."

13

FREY

KEANE'S FEET DIDN'T MOVE FORWARD, BUT HE TWITCHED WITH an apparent urge to go after Liana. "The Second is mine. I will cut him in threes before you leave here with him."

"Threes?" Liana considered it, perusing Chevelle where he stood, sword in hand. She was no fool, but Liana couldn't have predicted I would name him my Second when she'd made the bargain. That was merely an unexpected bonus to a deal that would be sweet for his other ties to me. She shook her head. "Not today, thank you. I need him for a few tasks first."

"Changeling," Keane warned, but his argument was cut short when Liana flicked a gaze beside him.

"Not today," she repeated, her words growing stronger as several tall, olive-skinned high fey in decorative leather armor weaved among those waiting. They positioned themselves nearer Keane, crossing their arms and sharing glances. They didn't move to touch the fire fey, but the intention was plain enough: they might die in the process, but given the chance, they would knock him from his protections and into the mercy of an elven lord and a changeling fey skilled in the art of killing.

Liana had put high fey in place. Liana had known.

"Take the Second," Keane said, glancing sidelong at Liana's fey, wordlessly promising a slow death before his eyes came back to Liana, "and I shall take a higher prize."

His meaning was clear. The only one of us a bigger prize than my Second was me. I stepped forward, feeling the pull on my magic, knowing every high fey in that field understood the full extent of what was happening. "I will not be bartered like a common stone. I come to see the lord of your high court, and if you think I would be so easily taken, you are all fools."

They weren't fools—they had strung out an endless array of traps and snares, magic and spellcasting. It was not some minor trick. They hadn't merely knocked us from our horses and muddied our faces. They'd used serious magic to get us there, planning and plotting for the series of events that would throw us off our normal response. *How long had they been preparing for this—since I'd been restored to the throne? Before that? Before Asher, even? Before the massacre?* My stomach turned.

I walked forward, unsure what would happen when I crossed the boundary, still tied within the grasp of countless fey, my magic tethered by both. It was possible that the protections set would sever the tie, release my power to me, and allow me to reach Chevelle and retaliate without risk. It was more likely that the fey had thought of that and my plan would backfire, releasing untold power to Keane and his underlings, who, with that kind of unchecked strength, would eventually end up destroying the entirety of both the fey and elven lands.

My confidence wavered at the thought, and I looked to the others. Liana stilled me with a glance, her smile opposing the warning meant only for me. She brushed some invisible dust from her dress, the shade of the fabric flickering briefly to green. Beyond her, Chevelle watched Keane, which was possibly more telling than Liana's response. My feet were frozen to the earth. I hated being trapped, and I hated not being able to help my guard.

I glanced at the lowering sun in a sky full of red. "Keane, you've wasted enough of my time. Carry on before I have my guard dispatch you."

He leaned forward, ready with a response. It was going to hurt.

Liana smiled and flicked her wrist. A half-dozen of the olive-skinned fey lunged, their long fingers digging into Keane's armor as they spun around him in tandem, pulling to knock him from his feet. The air exploded into flame, whirling through the fey and overhead as a hundred others looked on. *Do they have so much confidence in him? Or is it lack of devotion that keeps them rooted in place?*

A fire fey let loose a high-pitched howl, the sound screaming through the open field and inciting action. The rest of the line writhed and thrashed, clearly wanting to join in, but something was stopping them. It was as if they were tethered to their spots like I was.

The wind fell, and Keane shoved a fierce blast of power out from his position, collapsing Liana's fey into hissing, bubbling heaps. The anger on his face was hotter than that fire, and Liana laughed with a full-on cackle, complete with bending and pressing a hand to her chest. Keane's eyes narrowed, still hot with flame, and the line of fey stared at the broken men surrounding their chief.

Liana wiped at her cheek, brushing away phantom tears as her laughter died to a soft chuckle. "Priceless," she said. "And so easily won."

I had no idea what she was talking about, but Chevelle,

apparently at least suspicious of another plot, shot his gaze to her. She had warned me against spilling the blood of the high fey, but I wondered whether that was that a clue or another secret, some trickery of a changeling fey.

"Your flesh will shroud this stone, Liana, before three solid moons. That I can swear to you." Keane's tone had gone serious, but Liana's chin only tilted down, her gaze targeted on his. She was making promises of her own.

Chevelle straightened, sliding his belt into place but keeping his sword in hand. He could not come back to me or retreat over the barrier without it being an open win for the fey, an invitation to come at him full-force without regard to their own rules, but it was clear he was done. He meant no more fooling with the lot of them. Grey had sidled up beside him, edging out the few remaining fey who still waited amongst my guard, and I could finally see Rider, his scuffed black boots still against the stone and clay. Anvil's form blocked the rest of him from view, but he remained close, the toe of his own boots resting against his downed comrade's side.

I took a deep breath with little hope I could get us all out alive, but I was ready to make my bargain. "So," Liana said, cutting me off with a casual gesture toward the trees. "Let us go now, before the nightthings come calling." She turned to Keane, giving him a small nod. "Until then."

I hadn't the slightest idea how she meant to gather me, given that she'd just warned me about moving forward and the others could not move back, but Keane's reply stilled the shifting field once more.

"I'm afraid you're mistaken," he called to her. She caught my eye before glancing over her shoulder at her opponent, who remained in his small patch of land, protected from spellcasting and from magic.

"I don't believe that was ever the case," she purred.

He laughed mirthlessly before pointing to the ground at my guards' feet. "Then you are doubly mistaken, young one, because the blood that was spilled was not merely from those you owned."

Liana didn't look where he gestured, only at Keane. "Those were direct attacks. I wouldn't count them so eagerly."

He smirked, knowing her men had attacked him as well. "We simply intended capture, by my word."

Anvil stiffened at the mocking tone the fire fey had taken, the phrase "by my word" stolen from elven lands and bantered about like children at play. Anvil knew the word of the fey held no honor. He glanced back at me then leaned down to grip Rider by the belts crossing his waist and chest. I stared on as the large man lifted his friend, heaving him in one try across a shoulder.

"As I was saying," Liana said. "We shall go now."

The waiting fey grew restless, fire and wind igniting their line. She flipped a hand at them, but their magic only flickered.

They were going to move on us. There must have been some edict set forth, some warning about spilling the blood of the high fey, and it must have been on fey lands, not the ones we'd encountered in the castle.

Chevelle and the others had indeed spilled blood here, but so had Keane. I felt the tension growing wild inside me, filled with the need to act and my fear of those tethers tied beneath the earth. At least some of them would have to let go to attack me.

Liana kept moving, without worry by all outward appearance, but her shade had gone darker, tinged with hints of her own true hue.

"Kill them," Keane ordered, and though I couldn't be sure

precisely who the fey counted as targets, there was an immediate pull on the power within me. For an instant, I thought it was mine, a reaction to his words and a desire to fight. But it wasn't. It was them. The long line of fey standing before us drew my power through a sieve, tugging and tearing and willing it to them through the barrier to use against my own men. I fought it, clawing helplessly at the air and drawing every part of myself in. Someone called to me, but my ears were a roar of magic and power, the screaming wind, the fire, and then the shattering rock beneath my skin.

I was on the ground.

"I said *halt*," the voice commanded. A burst of power laced with the scent of leaves and the warmth of the summer sun shot through me. My teeth were gritted so hard they ached, and my leather-covered knees pressed into the shards of broken stone among water that had turned to ice. My hands shook, fingers crooked into hooks as they still fought an invisible battle.

But the tearing had stopped. No one was pulling on the ties. The clearing was silent.

I breathed. "Veil." His name came automatically, falling from my lips of its own accord as he stood suddenly in the clearing, his golden wings and golden skin shining like the sun in the lowering sky. His chest heaved, his breath coming faster than I thought I'd ever seen it. I wondered what he'd done to still the field and the two hundred fey. My eyes found Chevelle. Grey. Anvil. Rider.

Keane roared from his spot on the sidelines, and several of the younger fey retreated at the sound. "You've no right to enter this quarrel!"

Veil straightened, his gaze finally leaving me, making me aware that my hands remained frozen, outstretched, and struggling to not release my power. He had to understand what was happening. He had warned me.

"Elfreda, Lord of the North and the Dark Elves' Kingdom, is my guest, Keane. I assure you it is entirely my right, and I dare you to extend this quarrel one single beat of your darkened heart."

Veil's words were not the quiet warning I was used to. His speech was filled with danger, and the charge of electricity crawled up my skin, even over the barrier that separated us. It was the first time I'd noticed the heliotropes, Flora and Virtue, hovering outside the circle of blood and ash. They could control the whole scene if they wanted to. They could regain order if it was at Veil's hand.

Keane glared. "You count me as a fool? She does not cross unguarded upon your invitation."

Veil stepped forward, his shoulders and wings glistening not just with sun, but something damp. It covered his heliotropes as well. "Lord Freya is here upon my invitation."

Liana giggled, her thin hand smacking over an open grin at the turn of events. Everyone knew it wasn't an accident—the sound had been purposefully spelled from her. Veil gave the changeling a sidelong glance then gestured at me. "Come, Elfreda. We have business to attend to."

My breath caught in my throat. Liana's gaze flicked between Veil and me. I couldn't let go of the power. "I insist on safe passage," I answered after a moment, "for my guard." My heart tightened in my chest, but I refused to allow it hope. "And retribution for our injured. Upon my crown."

Veil looked at Rider strung over Anvil's shoulder. He pressed his lips together. Liana jerked her head toward the fallen fey at Keane's feet, but I could see only her back and wasn't certain what other clue she might have given.

Keane didn't wait for Veil's reply. "If the Lord of the Dark Elves claims retribution, then so do I."

There were more than a few high fey scattered about the battlefield that surrounded my guard, but I doubted Keane truly cared for their fate. What he was worried about, what *I* was worried about, was the release of my power from his other high fey.

Veil sighed. "What is your price?"

Keane and I spoke at the same time and though I said only, "Keane," he listed the names of my Seven. I did not miss that he'd excluded Ruby. I refused to let myself think it could be because they had already taken her head.

Liana raised a finger, her skin ethereal in its new glow. "Pardon the interruption, but that one"—her finger purposefully moved to point out Chevelle—"is mine." She smiled. "Legal and binding and bargained prior to the return of the North."

Veil shook his head. "How long do you need him?"

Liana shrugged and waggled her hand.

"Bring this to court," Veil ordered, his gaze sweeping the line of high fey. "The fates will decide."

I choked on a gasp. *Court. I might rather die right there.*

"Freya," Veil said. "With me."

No, I thought, *that is the worst thing that could happen.*

Liana latched on to Chevelle, grinning wildly, but he had gone still. There was nothing we could do. We could not allow my power to go to Keane. We could not allow him or any of the fey control of the Seven. We had to save Rider, we had to save Ruby. We had to stay alive. We were in a ball precariously perched on the end of a needle, and if not for Veil and his heliotropes, if not for Liana, we would all be lost. But Chevelle did not move.

His chest was frozen, his eyes unblinking as they focused beyond me. He might have been considering a way out, deciding how to destroy our problems, or contemplating anything. But I had known Chevelle all of my life, and if there was one thing I was sure of, it was that stillness was bad.

I'm sorry, I wanted to tell him. *I should have never let this come to be*. But I couldn't say anything. I couldn't even move.

"I—I will wait for safe passage," I told Veil.

His gaze rolled heavenward before addressing the line of high fey. "Disperse!" He flicked a warning glance at Keane, but I knew Keane wouldn't move from his protections until we were long gone.

Flora and Virtue drew their swords, a threat to the line of high fey. The ties within my magic were plucked like lute strings, the power reverberating as each separate connection was pulled free.

There had been more of them than I'd imaged.

I watched Chevelle, the bile in my stomach rising as each of the high fey set me free and the line turned to move away. Asher had given me too much power to even wield safely, and on fey lands, I could use none of it. I was powerless to help my family, to help my Second.

"Come," Liana whispered, pulling Chevelle with her in the opposite direction of Keane. I gestured for Anvil to follow. He and Grey would be safer with the changeling fey than with me.

The last of the high fey released my power, and it was drawn back into me, leaving every part of me exhausted and weak. Chevelle's eyes stayed on me even as the heliotropes took hold of me at each side. *Don't fight this*, I willed him. *It's your only way out*.

He took a breath then, and my feet lifted from the ground.

Above us, Veil waited, his golden wings turning a sickly hue in the setting sun. For the first time since I was a child, I was heading toward the fey court.

Alone. In the dark night.

FREY

The fey court was everything I remembered it to be. Narrow-trunked birch trees climbed high into the sky, their silver-white bark a wide ring arching around the center stage. They towered over the keystones, moonlight sparking off of both. If I was glad of anything, it was that we were not in the cover of the trees, under the canopy of the fey forests during the dark night. But I couldn't be grateful, not given the shape of those stones and the way they reached, slender and sculpted, toward the moon above. I didn't look at the points of their forms, the way the stone split like fingers, curling, pleading, at the sky in eternal agony. I only allowed myself to see the flowers, the fruited vines and thornless lianas trailing over and through the flat rocks that made up the arena's floor.

"Why did you bring me here?" I asked Veil, not turning to look at him. The heliotropes had given me my feet and moved back, but not out of earshot. They would need to protect me because beyond that ring of trees in a dense, unnatural forest waited countless fey, eager for blood.

Veil shifted behind me, not close enough that I could feel

his heat but enough that his scent mingled with the lush spectrum of flowers. "You know why."

Ceremony and spectacle were the cornerstones of the fey court's system. From the outside, it might not have seemed so different from our own, given the need for order, for a show of power, and to shut down those who might break its law. But the fey court was nothing like our land, and even Asher's brutal rule paled in comparison to the displays put on there. "It's too late for your tactics," I told him. "You've sentenced us to death."

Veil stepped beside me, his amber wing brushing the metal that adorned my side. He wouldn't have done that with his bare skin—not even Veil would tolerate the burn voluntarily, not when it might negate even a modicum of his power. "You misjudge me, Lord Freya. All the more so when I've offered you a trade."

I glanced over at him, leaving the shadows to dance through the trees unobserved. "Why have they taken her?"

Veil's mouth tightened, his hand coming to my waist to spin me once more toward the center stones. It wasn't for me. It was for those hidden within the darkness. "Court will come to session," he called, "in three days and upon the solid moon."

The trees erupted with lesser fey, like a covey of partridge startled from brush. They took to the sky, swirling and screeching on their way through the open air. They cut hard and fast into the deeper parts of the forest, spreading the word to masters and foes alike. It was their purpose, an assembly of court the highest possible priority.

It was the worst thing that could have happened. In a matter of hours, this court would start filling with fey of all types. They would fight and drink and bring out their best potions and poisons to share. There would be trades. There would be killings. It would be the biggest event to happen in ages, for among the trials would be an elven lord and her power, free for the taking.

"It's going to be a massacre," I told the empty arena.

"Yes," Veil answered. "But one under my hand."

I didn't reply because even though Veil held court, he would not have true control over the fey. He was merely at the helm, steering a ship among storm and sea.

"Come," he offered, guiding me by the elbow away from the arena's telling stones. "We shall rest amid the comforts of my home."

Worse, I thought. *Every moment, worse and worse.*

CHEVELLE

CHEVELLE HAD THREE DAYS TO RETURN TO COURT, THREE DAYS until the moon was solid and the fates would decide.

It was too long, and it wouldn't be long enough. He wanted to strangle Liana, to wring her cursed changeling neck.

"Hush now," she told him, apparently aware of his building aggression despite the fact he'd managed to bite his tongue thus far. "Let us get clear of the plain first."

She'd known the price. From the beginning, she'd led them all to that point. Not everything could be accounted for, and he suspected a few circumstances had simply fallen into place of their own accord, but Chevelle didn't believe in luck. Liana had known what Freya meant to him, even when he hadn't been her Second, even before she'd become Lord of the North. It might have happened unexpectedly and without preamble, but it wasn't chance. It was not the fates at play.

He'd been taken prey by a changeling, and it was going to cost him everything.

"She was not part of the gamble," he hissed at Liana. It had been signed expressly into their bargain. He would never have risked her so.

Liana glanced at him sidelong, her strides outpacing his as Grey and Anvil lagged behind. "I told her not to go after them. I said to leave the halfling to her fate."

"You knew she'd never let that happen. This is worse"—he faltered, refusing to imagine what would take place at the end of these three days—"this is worse than before."

Liana's skin flickered an ugly shade of green. "If you would simply stop her from making ill-met decisions and twisting the fates around—"

Chevelle's grip on his sword tightened, and Liana spoke more softly, flipping her hand through the air as if it was all of no consequence. "What is done is done. It doesn't matter. We have what we need to restore her. The boy has the key to get her back."

The boy. Steed. Chevelle's jaw clenched before he spat, "That *boy* is lying near dead in the castle. It's a day's ride from here, even if he were well." He was losing his cool with the changeling and thought there might only be one fey who tested him more. He wouldn't think of the other, the one who had Freya and was carrying her in the opposite direction of the path he walked. Leaving her.

Liana's grin was wry. "Have you learned nothing from me, Vattier?"

Chevelle recognized something in her tone, and it caused him to draw short on his anger. It made him think, just for a moment, that maybe they did have a chance. In all of his years, Liana had been the only person who pronounced his family's name so, as if it was just a designation and not a nasty series of events to be mocked or scorned, to be whispered. It was not the things that Asher had done, the rumors and secrets that surrounded a mother who had been cast out by the crown and the shame of a father who had pledged fealty to that same crown. Liana wasn't elven, so she didn't truly care about their politics or who he was. She wanted something, simple as that, and restoring Frey to the throne was the only way to get it.

That didn't mean he trusted her. "It will stay in my possession until the moment we make the trade."

Liana smiled, and it seemed genuine. "I would hope so. *I'd* never be fool enough to trade with a fey at court."

RUBY

RUBY AWOKE WITH A SPLITTING HEADACHE AND TWO SHARP needs. The first was the desire for water, because she couldn't remember the last time she'd had anything to drink. The second was the strongest of the two, but she'd have to tamp down the desire for revenge. And once she'd done that, well, there was no telling when she would get a drink.

The ring of trees surrounding them was dark, their jagged leaves blocking the moon. It was there, she knew it was, and it would be nearly full. "Rhys," she hissed, her voice hoarser than she thought it should have been. She hoped that didn't mean she'd been asleep longer than she'd estimated.

"Rhys," she hissed again, throwing an elbow into his ribs before the ropes tying her stopped the move. She'd made contact, though, and Rhys groaned and coughed. "Shake it off," she whispered, nudging him awake. "We have two days, three at most."

His lifted his head to reveal nearly closed, puffy eyes. He didn't speak, but his expression asked, *Three days to what?*

She jerked her chin toward the sky. "The solid moon.

When the fates dance."

Rhys flinched, his squinting eyes finding the circle of stones, their elf-like forms turned down, curled in among themselves, their hands covering their faces and mouths in eternal screams. Shadows shifted among them, lesser fey skittering into the cover of oversized leaves when their guards made any sign of movement.

"We have to get out of here," Ruby told Rhys. "And it has to be by tomorrow's dawn."

A screech came from the trees above from lesser fey suddenly jerking on the ropes and woven chains that bound them together and in the air. Acorns plinked off the stone beneath them, bouncing toward the guards' feet. The air smelled of moist earth and ferns, of lilac and lavender and deep forest moss. Ruby breathed in every scent, searching for any that might be of use. All she caught were more and more of the feylings, acrid and pungent and itching for what was to come.

They were well and truly done for, and it made venom bite at her tongue.

One of the guards stood, his glossy skin covered in sturdy armor. He narrowed his eyes at the offending sprite in the trees above, and then the sounds of the feyling's scuffling and broken grunts were cut short. It didn't fall to the ground, so Ruby could only assume the guard had tied the thing in place. One more acorn plinked onto the stones, but the forest was otherwise silent.

"What are your orders?" Ruby called to the closest guard. "I mean aside from watching us hang?"

He ignored her, as he'd done to the various high fey spectators waiting in the trees—twenty of them, she estimated, watching and hoping to catch some glimpse of the action to come.

They wanted to see the halfling fey.

Her mouth tightened automatically, and she could feel the burn of her skin against the spelled ropes. She'd never get out that way—anger would only get her hurt. Fire wouldn't win any battles in that world. "You know, I've trained for this," she told him flatly. "For all my years, I've known this day would come."

The guard didn't turn his head, but she could tell he listened. He said so in the cock of his chin and the tension of his spear arm.

"That bit with the others was just for show. I wanted to get here, needed to be near him. You see that, don't you? You can sense it in your bones?" She whispered the last bit, letting it feel like their secret.

The guard stood still, breathing slowly and evenly. He didn't scan the tree line, didn't skirt the stones, only stared into the distant shadows.

She knew she was getting to him. No one wanted to anger the keeper. She knew they were all tense, second-guessing every decision. It was too big a game, and the stakes were too significant.

"No matter," she told him. "It'll all be over soon." She sighed as regretfully as she could and glanced at Rhys where he hung beside her. She didn't think she'd ever seen him so annoyed. She grinned and bumped him with her elbow.

Her eyes returned to the guard, her smile the only weapon she had left. "Personally, I cannot wait."

Rhys sighed and straightened, apparently resigned to follow whatever path she had in mind. His armor had been stripped off him, likely dumped in the forest along their way. His black cloth shirt had weathered it well, though, and neatly crisscrossed rope took the place of a once well-supplied array of leather holsters. She was glad their captors had tied her and

Rhys so closely and that the dried latticework of vine behind them allowed her to see movements that he or the guards made, but knowing what else was behind the trees would have helped. It was dark night in that forest, the most dangerous stretch of time in fey lands. It made it hard to make a good assessment regarding their escape, and she wished she had a better idea what awaited them behind which tree. Rhys's hand shifted against the knotted twine, and she had the feeling things were about to get sticky.

"Ha!" she shouted, hoping to distract at least one of the guards, but before she got another word out, she was suddenly falling, twisting, hurtling upside down through the air. She had a moment of weightless panic, and then she was laughing, realizing what Rhys had done. He had a weapon, and it wasn't just metal—it had been spelled against fey magic.

Her Seven had been ready for battle. She was breathless, and the laughter was real—a full thrill of the hunt had taken over, and instinct threw her hands skyward into a flip as Rhys cut the last rope free. She landed in somersaults, tumbling toward the closest guard, who was within reach. Her slim boots wrapped around him, hands slithering under his arm and over his neck as they dragged tangles of broken rope along. The tug on her raw wrists was background noise to the rest of her senses. Her eyes counted the dangers, picking off guards one by one. Her hearing had gone sharp, singling out threats among the cheering crowd.

Rhys slid down the web of ropes with the slender blade he'd somehow managed to keep at his side. The forest was screaming around them, lesser fey screeching and squawking like a river of birds. The trees came alive with fire, but it wasn't Ruby's—it was their theatre, and the halfling fey was their prize.

"Behind you!" Rhys shouted, drawing her free of that

single-minded focus and the fury of the gathering multitude. She was of the Seven—she didn't fight for herself alone. She slid over the guard she'd been holding, leaving his back where hers had been. She was moving, using her arms and legs and fire as both shields and weapons as the need to escape and the call for revenge spurred her on. A conflagration had lit the clearing, the stone structures dark and eerie as their shadows danced in flame. It was why they were leaving. This was not how she would end, as stone frozen for eternity in the dark mirror of the fey high court.

"Three!" Ruby shouted over her shoulder, warning Rhys of the new guards who seemed to materialize out of the trees. He moved, but not as fast as he should have. The flame was too hot for him, and she knew the smoke clouded his eyes and filled his lungs. She cursed and spun backward, edging close to him while fighting her own way through. Two of the high fey took flight, but she couldn't tell if they were headed for backup or to find a better vantage point to fight. More and more and more appeared—there were too many. She needed her magic. She needed a true weapon.

Rhys's blade was slick with blood, and his unarmored chest and legs were soaked, too, with both his and that of the fey. She reached for him, pressing a hand to his side as they fought back to back and urging him toward what was left of those burning trees. It was dark in the cover of the forest, and there were too many fey to make a clean break, but none of that would matter if she didn't keep Rhys alive. Her own eyes began to water, the smoke in the clearing thick and noxious, but a cold wind swept through, bringing air scented with violet and lily blossoms. It was entirely out of place and swiftly overtaken by horehound and amaranth.

"Move," she told Rhys, reaching out with her magic to the pulsing energy that lay beneath the earth. She'd tried before, but she couldn't draw on it, and she spat a curse, a little blood, and an order for him to lie flat on the ground. He obeyed her or passed out from lack of air—she wasn't sure—as she pulled a living vine from the canopy beyond them that had yet to burn to its death.

It was a whip, hard and fast and laced with thorns when she shoved her magic into it. Her wrist was battered and her body weak, but she snapped it, hooking the vine around one guard's leg to yank it solidly from beneath him and then again as soon as it curled free. A staff struck out, barely missing her as a spear grazed her leg. She swung the whip above her and forward. Though it lacked the bite of her own and its metal spikes, it could pull a fey from the air. It could give her a breath and a second to plan ahead. It could get them off the blasted ground and into the trees.

She flicked the whip upward, rolling down and over Rhys's form. The whip struck the fey above her, biting at it only enough to annoy and infuriate, and she wrapped an arm and a vine around Rhys's body. Her power pulsed through her as she shoved the vine and its claws high into the trees. It caught a limb and dug in, and Ruby was moving once more. Two fey sliced at her magic, but the vine grew swiftly with the last of her effort. She would get them to safety. She would do at least that one single thing.

Ruby was panting and gritting her teeth, but the air had become cleaner, and Rhys choked in several full breaths. He shoved the short handle of his blade into her palm and took hold of the vine, drawing them both higher into the trees. She wrapped a quick knot around the dagger, and her new whip was suddenly a true weapon, spelled metal, magic and steel. She grinned again, certain it was an ugly thing, and then swung.

She'd nearly started to believe it might work when the air was swept from the clearing.

She gasped, gulping for a breath that wasn't there, watching with sinking hope as all the smoke and fire was swallowed into nothing, sucked into some invisible space that left their battlefield dark and silent. When she finally got her breath again, she had nothing to say.

Rhys said it for her: "Pitt."

He said it in the way one said an epitaph, but Pitt wasn't dead. He was there, cold and colorless, the most beautiful and terrible thing Ruby had ever seen. Her grip went slack on the makeshift handle of the vine—there was no need for a weapon when one's opponent could not be beaten. He was the most powerful changeling among the fey, and there he was, close enough to the source of fey energy that even with her weapons, she would not have stood a chance. The chatter of the feylings had died with Pitt's entrance, but it began to rise again, a giggling current of celebration and half-formed words. It didn't matter how things went. They were in for a show. The high fey were quiet, though, and not as careless with their actions in the presence of the new creature. A good show was well and fine, as long as they weren't the ones punished at the hands of the keeper.

The changelings were truly fey, Ruby supposed, but she had never felt any sort of kinship to their line. She couldn't imagine it, unable to believe that part of her blood could in any way be similar to a being like that.

"Halfling," Pitt mused, "I hope you don't intend to leave before the festivities even begin."

Ruby swallowed her first response. If Veil was attractive, Pitt was pure temptation. There was no strut to him, no grandeur or show. He didn't need it. He was fascinating and captivating, a specimen of pure pleasure and allure.

Ruby despised him. She wiped her bloodied palm on her pant leg. She wouldn't be afraid of him. "What do you want of me, changeling?"

He laughed in a broken huff of air. His dark eyes never came away from her, never took notice of the watching crowd. He never seemed to care that Rhys, an elven lord's high guard, stood at her flank. Pitt's head tilted to the side as he examined her, far longer than was strictly necessary.

She shook her head. "Swine."

His skin flicked a few shades warmer, mirroring Ruby's fair tone. His spiky white hair slowly went metallic, somehow making the slant of his ears and the line of his neck more interesting. Subtle as it was, the action seemed to say he could be like her—he could be fire. But he would never be like Ruby. And that was why they wanted her.

"You know I'll always have the upper hand," she told Pitt. It was true, but only by the furthest stretch, and only with regard to her gift, because everyone knew a changeling fey would rather be strung inside out from the trees of Hollow Forest than allow themselves to be bested. He would turn her to stone and keep her forever before he let her win.

She refused to look at the monstrous sculptures scattered through the clearing. Instead, she stared at Pitt, the dark eyes that narrowed and shifted as she watched them, the long fingers that curled around his oaken spear. He was all lean muscle, but Ruby knew talons waited beneath. "I have something you don't," she continued, the weight of Rhys beside her making her less brave. She could not lose him for her own loose tongue. "Stringing me up won't get it."

Pitt waited, his expression eager.

Ruby couldn't know if it was for her words or her blood. She straightened, facing him full-on. "I propose a trade."

STEED

S{\sc teed's} {\sc thoughts were slow and sticky}. H{\sc e'd been injured} a time or two before. He knew Thea's healing method, and what was happening was not it. There was something terribly wrong, but he couldn't quite bring to mind what.

"Thea," he started, pushing against the solidness of the table. He didn't know what he was doing there, why he wasn't in his rooms, or where everyone—*anyone*—else was.

He wobbled, and Thea's hand shot out to catch him. His skin tingled with reminders of tonic and potions, recently rinsed clean. He remembered Thea doing so and, in turn, the question he'd drawn short on only heartbeats before. But there was something else, some nagging, urgent compulsion that he couldn't quite place. There was something he needed to do.

He shook his head, reaching gingerly for a shirt as she held his arm. He glanced down at her, the height of the table putting them closer to eye to eye than he'd ever recalled being. But no, it wasn't merely the table causing that. Thea had grown.

His hand reached out to touch her, brushing the skin over her cheekbone. The scar that sat below the corner of that eye had faded, probably not noticeable to anyone who wasn't looking for it. But Steed knew Thea, at least he *had* known her once. It had been ages.

"Why are you here?" His words came out harsher than he'd meant them, such an odd juxtaposition to his touch. He was touching her. He snapped his hand back, nodded an apology, and shook his head again. He needed something to drink, anything that would wash the poison away.

"I've come to visit you," she told him. Her voice was low, somehow an apology in itself, and then she turned to pour clean water into a smooth stoneware cup. "You weren't well, so I offered to stay with you." She handed him the earthen mug, and its surface felt too smooth, too cold against the haze that surrounded him. "To help you get back on your feet."

He set the cup on the table then slid the shirt over his head. It felt like a thousand blades in his side, as if a spiked chain was being dragged from chest to shoulder.

"May I?" she asked him, indicating the laces of his shirt with a tip of her head. It was only a courtesy, as she'd apparently already done far more with whatever treatments had him so deep in his fog.

Her fingers were thin and nimble, making quick work of the ties. She handed him the cup again, as if she simply knew he needed to drink. He held it longer the second time, taking in the narrow room and its scents and the bars on the door.

"I appreciate what you've done for me," he told her, "but there's something I need to do." He would be damned if he could figure out what it was, though.

She placed her fingers over the skin of his forearm, and the touch seemed a thousand degrees warmer than the cup in his hand. "Stay with me a moment longer," she said. "I've come all this way just to call on my old friends."

His eyes fell to her hand on his arm, which was not quite a restraint, but a ready grip. He set the icy cup on the table beside him. "No. That's not why you've come."

She blushed—or flushed—it was hard to tell with Thea.

He suspected anger over chagrin, despite the lightness of her tone.

"You're right," she confessed. Her voice went gentle, all honest concession to anyone who didn't know better. "I got restless." She sighed, absently brushing a long, dark lock away from her neck. He couldn't remember when she'd taken her hair down or how long he'd been holding her hand.

"I wanted something different," she told him. Her eyes were deep brown, framed by thick lashes. She used them well, lowering her head to look through them. Sometimes, Thea's eyes smiled when she didn't.

Steed liked a girl who could smile, one who could cut his heart with her laugh.

"Didn't you ever feel that? The need to fit in, to be useful. To make your mark."

The cup was in his hand again, but he hadn't forgotten the scent marking it. Thea's presence meant it was sleight of hand. "You're lying, Thea. I may be under a tonic, but I know you at least that well."

She colored, definitely in a flush of irritation. Her eyes narrowed. "Take your medicine, Summit."

He knocked the cup to the floor.

Her gaze never left his. "There's more where that came from."

He stood.

She straightened.

He fell.

Thea grunted, going forward and nearly to her knees to catch him in time. "Oh for the love of—why can't you just behave, you stubborn—"

He leaned on her hard, closing his eyes against the spin. "Don't talk to me like your livestock," he murmured. There was no vehemence in the words anymore. He needed her. He needed—*something*. "I have a thing I need to do," he told her. He knew it was enormously important.

"Aye, I suppose you do," she answered. She hefted him up, propping them both against the table, and leaned back to appraise him.

His mouth pulled up into an unsteady grin, an assurance that might have been a lie.

She pointed a finger at him, at the grin. "You'd better behave, or it's right back on the table with you, potion and all."

"Water," he said. "And I promise."

She glanced at the cup again, but Steed stopped her with a word. "Ruby." He meant to explain, but he was bringing up the past to someone who'd known them both. It felt good to say it —it was somehow important. "All the tonics and elixirs. She's been sneaking them in my drinks for years, a bit in food, a bit on my skin." He laughed. "Oh, but we had a row of it, fighting and bickering every spring when the plants were new and her mixes at their strongest. 'You have to trust me,' she'd say. 'It'll be worth it in the end.'"

Thea's mouth had gone slack, but it wasn't at the description of Ruby building up Steed's tolerance to potions. It was the something else.

"Ruby," he said. "Ruby, Ruby, Ruby." That was the thing, the nagging something he needed to do. He regarded Thea's face. "Where is she?"

Thea's jaw snapped shut, her eyes darting around the room, but it was too late. His memory was returning.

The tonics were too weak, which meant they weren't Ruby's tonics.

Thea must have seen the realization in his expression, for her hands went up, palms out, and she backed away slowly, corralling him. "Stay calm," she told him. "Just wait here for a bit and—"

"Thea," he started.

"No."

He took a step forward, unsteady despite his advantage against the drugs. "Where is Ruby? What happened?"

The pain in his side was suddenly sharper, jolted by moving, and he remembered a golden fey and a knife tipped with poison. He remembered the scream. The armored forms of seven spiders. The library. The book. His sister.

"Ruby," he said again. "Ruby, Ruby, Ruby." He forced the memories to come back, every terrible image leading him to another. Then he had the awful, awful truth: they had her.

"Water," he ordered. Thea didn't move straight away, and he could tell she was considering another attempt at sneaking him the drugged drink. "We need to help her. We have to go. We have to—"

Thea shook her head. "You don't understand. While you were injured, Liana—"

Steed stopped her again. "Liana was here?"

Thea's shoulders came up, her face in a helpless grimace. She pointed at his side.

"Liana placed this tonic on me."

Thea nodded.

"For Frey."

"What?"

Steed shook it off, waving a hand toward the basin. "That doesn't matter. Clean water, now. We need to go."

She did as he asked but questioned him as she went. "Go

where? You don't even know where to look for her. What are you planning to do?"

Her implied *in your condition* was the least of his concern, but he needed a plan, some idea of what he actually intended to do… He considered for a long moment, the fog still heavy in his mind and through his senses. "Junnie," he said. "We have to find Junnie."

THEA

THEY SHOULDN'T HAVE LEFT THE CASTLE. SHE NEVER SHOULD have let them.

It was too late, she knew even as she glanced nervously over her shoulder, even as the other sentries—a few dozen of Edan's most experienced men—watched the forest for them.

"I don't understand," Steed told her, "how it is that *you* know where Junnie is."

Thea's attention came back to her charge, her patient—her superior, since she was a castle sentry in training. She wasn't sure how she got herself into such situations. "I know a lot of things, Summit. You're not the only one with spies."

He eyed her over the rim of a metal cup as she finished working on his side. "I don't have spies. If you mean Ruby, she never tells me anything." He put down the cup. "At least not anything I understand until it's too late, anyway."

He'd been chugging clean water from a hefty supply of canteens since they'd left the castle, but he'd still managed to fall from his horse twice due to the effects of the medicines. For any other man, tumbling from a moving animal might seem reasonable given the situation, but it was Steed. He was as comfortable on a horse as on his own feet.

"Fall one more time, and I'm not going to be able to stitch you back together. You're starting to look like shredded leather here."

He took a deep breath, shrugging his shirt back into place. He wore no plate or armor, but if they ended up where she was afraid they might, it wouldn't matter, anyway. Armor wouldn't be enough.

"Tell me," he said. "What do you know of Junnie and how to find her?"

She brushed a loose strand of hair from her face, gathering the sides to run a quick plait. She'd had no more than a second to prepare at the castle, not even a chance to draw breath for an explanation for the head of the guard, Edan. "She's going with me," Steed had ordered. There hadn't been much room for argument after that.

Steed snatched a piece of leather from her belt, offering it to her as he watched her tie the end of her braid. "You asked me why I was here," she answered, tucking the strip into itself and securing the hair in place. "That's why. Rumor of Junnie. Rumor of the rogues. Rumor of halfling fey. Something was coming, and though I didn't know precisely what, I knew I had to come."

Steed didn't seem surprised at the mention of the rogue bands becoming restless or the talk of halfling fey, so she knew he must have heard the same. But if he didn't know about Junnie, the rumors could be true. "They are worried about the child?" he asked her.

She nodded. "So now you know my secrets. Tell me yours. I'm about to risk my neck here, Summit. I'd like to know why."

"Ruby," he said simply.

"This isn't just about Ruby." She found herself pointing

that blasted finger at him again and forced it down. "The truth. I deserve it." She knew that he trusted her. If he'd had any obvious doubts about her, she never would have asked him to share them with her. But Steed wouldn't risk her safety. He would tell her if she was in over her head.

"You know how Ruby was brought into this world, about my father and a particularly devious fey?"

Thea nodded. She remembered Ruby's mother, even though she'd never met the fire fairy personally. It had been such a legend in Camber that she suspected anyone even passing through would have known. It wasn't just that that the fairy had seduced a recently widowed horse trader or that she'd managed one of the only successful halfling births in recent history, but the child she'd brought into being had come with a special gift. The girl was venomous, and the fey woman had paid for her treachery with her life.

"By all rights," Steed told her, "my sister never should have survived." He reached into his pocket, pulling out a leather-bound register wrapped in cloth. "But she did. And her mother named her Ruby." He patted the book, his strong hands dwarfing it. His eyes met hers. "Because she knew."

Thea opened her mouth to ask what it was the woman knew, but Steed was back on his feet. "Let's go," he told her. "We have a long ride to get there, even if Junnie has moved as close as you say."

Thea straightened to standing, shrugging her belt back into place and twisting her lip. "I hope you're right, Mister Summit. Because we're getting farther and farther from the castle with every galloped step."

Steed looked toward the mountain, the height of it disappearing beyond heavy fog. "It isn't the castle I'm worried about."

CHEVELLE

LIANA SCREAMED, NOT WITH THE SCREECH OF AN ANGRY WOMAN but with the soul-splitting scream of an ancient changeling who had planned and plotted and lost the key that would allow her to win. It was anger spelled to life.

Chevelle couldn't say he disagreed with her. "How long have they been gone?" he barked.

Edan glanced at the sky. "They could be near the base of the mountain by now, as long as the Summit boy keeps his seat."

Chevelle's eye narrowed on Edan, who quickly and obviously realized his mistake. Steed had taken to spending leisure time among the sentries, playing cards and betting stakes. They'd all become too casual. Despite his charm and easy humor, Steed was no boy. He was High Guard. He was one of their Seven. It was bloody well time he started acting like it.

"We'll never catch him," Grey said. "It's an extra day's ride, and even if they've stopped—"

"We could go on to court," Anvil offered. He gestured toward Liana, whose screaming had ceased and glass-breaking had commenced. "She could fly down there, grab whatever she needs from Steed—"

Liana picked up a stoneware pitcher and slammed it onto the library floor. "Is it so easy?" she chided. "Flit down there like a reeking pixie and snatch whatever I need? Are you a fool?"

Anvil shrugged. "I'm not the one who let him—"

Liana's finger shot up, pointing dangerously at Anvil's broad face. "Don't you say it."

"I'm going without you," Chevelle told her. "Do what you will, but I won't abandon her to the fey." They knew he meant Freya. He didn't need to say her name. He wasn't certain he could say it aloud, in any case.

"It's a fool's errand, and you know it," Liana shot back. "If you don't have the key, there's nothing for you to bargain."

"What is the key?" Grey asked her. "We'll have fake it. We'll do whatever needs to be done."

Liana sighed, her fingers curling into claws then straightening again. She was green beneath the eyes, the rest of her barely retaining her usual silvery gray. "It can't be faked. It isn't possible."

"You underestimate us," Grey said.

She smirked, and her testy fidgeting momentarily ceased. "That I do not. It isn't something you can fake. The key is laced with fey magic, with a *particular* fey's magic."

There was silence for a long moment, the hard truth of it sinking in. One couldn't counterfeit that kind of marking. It could only come from a few of the most powerful high fey. Chevelle had seen it once. "The diary," he said. "The key is the diary, marked by Ruby's mother. The fey want that journal."

Liana's eyes shot to Chevelle, apparently unaware that he had knowledge of the fey markings and appalled that he'd so easily named the key.

"Wait," Grey said.

But Chevelle was moving quickly and deliberately.

"Do you mean the one we carried with us, the one you bartered the stone for?" Grey said, hurrying to keep up. "*That* diary?"

"No," Chevelle answered. "They want Ruby's. Not Frey's."

He'd said it—he'd said her name, and it had not crushed him. Because he had a plan. It wasn't over.

Liana rushed in front of him, confusion slipping through her mask. "It isn't here. The Summit boy—"

"Anvil's right," he told her. "We will go on without Steed. We don't have time for anything else."

"But you'll never—"

"We've tried it your way," he answered. "It's done. You lost."

Liana drew up short, and the entire procession stopped to keep from running her down.

"Stay here if you want," he offered. "Heal Rider. Keep away from harm." He leaned forward, making it clear he was done playing her games. "It doesn't tally, Liana. We will do this our way because it's the only way they can't win."

"There isn't another diary," she whispered. "It has to be that which is marked."

Chevelle smiled. "And that's why I trust only Ruby." *Curses,* he thought, *she must have planned this ages ago, even as she fought for her own life beside us.* She'd kept it so much a secret that even Grey hadn't known two books existed. His chest was alight. He was ready to run all the way to the fey court. It hadn't been a lie. He *did* trust Ruby. There was a promise in his stare when it met Liana's. She would not win that bargain.

He trusted Ruby. "Even the half that is fey."

FREY

DAWN BROKE AT THE EDGE OF THE GREAT FOREST, TIPPING THE leaves with gold and red. I wasn't sure I had slept at all—my eyes were raw and muscles weary. My boots felt heavy on the glass-tiled floor, which threw reflections from the rising sun across every surface of the room.

Veil's home was all elegance, every bit of it impressive and lovely. I wanted to hate it. I wanted to be miserable and violent and curse him to his ruin. But I was tired. I felt beaten. I had been fooled into capture, submission, and a slow-and-painful death.

All I could see was sunshine, bright and blinding and touching every space of the open room. It was too warm. It felt too alive.

"I'll send for some food," Veil offered.

He'd been quiet all night, knowing I wasn't asleep as I sat rigidly against a plush amber chair. He hadn't spoken, though —he'd left me be but hadn't left me alone. It wouldn't have been safe there for an elven lord. The lure of having their own lasting legend would be worth the cost of death—or whatever horrible punishment was meted out by Veil—to too many of the fey.

"You know I won't eat it," I told him. "Not even from your private reserve."

He nodded, and I forced my gaze to move from the windowed view of the treetops to focus on him instead of that skyline, which was empty of mountains, empty of the place I called home. Empty was how I felt, too, hollow and alone, as if everything we'd been through had been for nothing. I felt as though I'd lost every single thing that mattered.

Flora and Virtue had left us, probably posting new patrols at early light, but the basin and supplies they'd brought in waited on a carved ivory table. "Clean up," Veil said. "We have work to do."

We would, wouldn't we? The coming days would be filled with preparation and planning. That was what the fey did. We would be seen. There would be presentations, the phases of the ceremony, and my skin was still caked with remnants of river clay and signs of battle. I couldn't make myself care.

"There is still a chance," he told me. "If you come with me now, let me show you—"

"A chance for what?" I snapped. "For you, for this court?" Life suddenly returned to my limbs, and I stood, my fists clenched and feet ready to fly. "For your kind to destroy everything on our side of the boundary?"

His mouth turned down in disapproval.

"Don't expect me to play nice here. Don't think I don't know how this works." I pointed a finger his direction, stepping forward without intending to do so. I could feel the power boiling within my palm, wanting to strike. "Don't think I don't know that you were aware of what was happening this entire time."

He waited for my anger to simmer down, watching me

with more patience and less of that usual suggestion of fascination or annoyance that seemed always on his face. We had no audience, so there was no need for a show. I was just a broken girl like my mother and hers before. It all started with emptiness and despair. Everyone knew how it ended.

"As such," he finally answered, "I trust that you will allow me to reveal what it is that I want."

"A bargain," I said flatly.

He smiled. "I do not assume you would fall so easily into that trap." He gestured toward the basin. "I only hope to appeal to the virtues that have allowed you to take rule. If you'll permit it, I believe there is good cause to share this truth with you." He let out a deep breath, and his eyes swept from the dirty slash on my forearm to my face. "As I said before, I would like you to consider this a mutually beneficial arrangement."

"Does it involve the release of my Seven and me?"

His gaze rolled toward the ornate high ceiling. "I'm afraid it may."

I stopped before a reply could come, the words frozen in my throat.

"It won't be easy," Veil told me. "But the best rewards never are."

"You're lying." My voice was low, tremulous. I wouldn't let myself believe. It was always a trick. It *had* to be a trick.

Veil laid a hand across his chest and inclined his head. "I will do my best to be honest with you, Lord Freya. Lacking that, you'll still have the use of your own eyes"—his gaze met mine once more—"if you will allow it."

"Where?"

He straightened, his smile thin. "Just beyond the trees."

≈

AFTER I'D RINSED my wounds and cleaned the blood and mud from my face, Veil had pasted syrup-soaked leaves over the deepest of my wounds. I didn't trust him or his remedies, but if he wanted to poison me, he had ample chance.

And then we were flying, with Veil in the lead while I was escorted by his heliotropes. A band of shadow stalkers wasn't far behind, and I wondered if they'd seen their brethren, the wounded soldiers who had stood waiting for my message to Veil. I had sliced their hands from their arms. It had been brutally violent. Every time I took such actions, it seemed necessary, but in the too-bright sky, the politics of it were far away, and it struck me that they were creatures, not so different than my birds.

I shook my head, forcing the thoughts away. I didn't like being so near the heliotropes—it was wearing on my ability to stay sane. I needed my feet beneath me, the ground. The fey were *not* like my birds.

The forest passed below us at dizzying speed, its color so lush and green that it made my time in the village seem like standing in a bed of dying weeds. The woodlands eventually fell into sparse patches of trees, though the earth was covered in brush and vines and everything green. The massive exotic leaves and the unusually-colored plants were gone, but it still resembled nothing I'd ever seen. The land lacked the roll of small hills, the cut of a curving stream. Despite the greenery, it was flat and lifeless, devoid of stone or the feel of fauna. I didn't think I'd ever been so far out into fey territory, but it didn't look as if they wandered out that way much, either. It felt abandoned, as though something was missing.

"What is this place?" I said to Flora, who held me at one side by the leather straps crossing my torso.

She didn't respond, but at my other side, the corner of Virtue's mouth turned down. Veil slowed, his gaze taking in the horizon, practically scouring it before meeting his heliotropes' eyes. Some unspoken message was exchanged, and the fey women lowered me to the ground.

My feet sank into soft, dry moss.

Flora and Virtue released their grip, and I straightened out my clothes as they returned to the sky with the dark-winged shadow stalkers. I felt the weight of them gone, as if I was lighter on my own two feet. I didn't want to fly, not like that.

There was still something not right about the ground. The undercurrent of the power that ran through the fey lands had changed.

Veil was at my side. "Come," he told me, his voice too low, somehow cautious. It was unlike him.

My knees locked.

"We mustn't waste time," he said. "The fates wait for no one."

The fates would dance at the fall of tomorrow's sun. It was the last of my time. It felt wrong. "I shouldn't be here," I said.

"Indeed, but you are." He touched my elbow, careful of the metal that had not been ripped from my armor during the battle. "Come with me, now."

And I did, despite all the reasons not to and despite the fact that my time was coming to an end. There was nothing to be done about any of it.

We walked carefully over land that seemed untouched by fey hands, the vegetation wild and undergrown. Moss bled into low grass, and small field mice and bugs skittered away from our boots. I hadn't seen any larger animals, but there would be birds in the low trees ahead—unfamiliar birds that might be harder to find, but birds nonetheless. I reached out for them, hesitant and unsure of the hold I had on that magic that seemed so intrinsic only to me. I had to correct myself, though, because it wasn't only me. It had been Junnie's. It had been my mother's, my aunt's—all the women in my family had the same magic.

"You understand why you're here, don't you?"

Veil's words startled me, and I nearly stumbled on a vine before my eyes went back to the ground to ensure safe footing. I didn't understand, not truly. I got his tactics, yes, but never Veil himself. I answered anyway. "Because of my power. If one of your kind is going to take me, you must take me first."

He couldn't allow an enemy to have that kind of supremacy. In spite of everything I'd hated about Asher, I couldn't say that Veil using the same methods, given his position, was wrong. My power falling into another fey's hands would destroy his realm, and that I did understand. I glanced over my shoulder, but the lithe forms of Flora and Virtue were nowhere in sight. "But not everyone approves."

Veil's eyes softened, the late-summer light giving them a honeyed-amber glow. "You know how we feel about your kind."

"Right," I said, annoyed despite myself. "So why warn me that Asher's guard Rowan was a threat to me, and that others planned to rise against me seasons ago? Why not just let them take care of it for you then?"

"The fey don't want any of Asher's half-bloods on the throne. You," he said, "are simply the lesser of his evils."

"Thanks."

"Be pleased I intervened at all," he said. "You and I both know what would have happened if a full-blooded fey had taken that throne."

"And what's to stop it from happening now? In three days"—no, it was two, I reminded myself. I had wasted one solid night doing nothing, waiting for it to come. I looked at Veil.

"It won't," Veil answered. "That's why we are here."

"Where?" I asked him. "*Where* are we?"

His breath was like a sigh, long and full of sorrow. He turned to the trees and gestured for me to lead the way.

A long line of braided trees marked the edge of a clearing, and the whisper of Veil's steps halted behind me. I kept walking, half-dried leaves crunching beneath my boots. I should have been searching for birds or scanning ahead for signs of whatever trap I might have been walking into, but the earth felt wrong, not fey enough. And then I froze, my heartbeat stuttering in one-two thumps before powering into thunder.

The high-fey lord stood silently behind me, but I knew Veil could see my panic. He waited, watching.

All I managed was a breathless, "*No.*"

LIANA

LIANA CURSED THAT WRETCHED ELF GIRL TO THE HILLS OF THE ice lands and back. Thea's tone echoed in her mind, that sharp and pointed argument coming back again. "You should know my name," she'd said. Well, yes, Liana did, and she would remember it.

Thea should have been the one to heal the elven guards, not running off with the key to Liana's plans, her fey bargain. Liana had more important tasks to take to hand, things that must be done before the dying light.

"Aaah," the dark-haired man beneath her palms said, and Liana drew her claws in as she pulled the bandage tighter.

"You've been stabbed," she told him. "I would tell you not to jostle about, but I'm certain you'll be headed into battle and will ignore my advice." She twisted his arm with one hand and pressed against his chest with the other to make certain the muscle wasn't too badly severed. "You are fortunate nothing is broken, but it was the blade of a spelled beast, and that magic will be crawling about in you for some time. Drink a bit of this." She handed him a bowl that burned even her accustomed senses. "Likely, it won't cure the matter, but it will keep you from noticing the effects as badly."

"What happened?" the man—Rider, she thought—asked his brethren.

She knew the other's name was Grey. He mattered—not to Liana, so much, but certainly to Liana's plan.

"It was a trap," Grey told him, "though I suppose you've gathered as much."

She had done what she could to heal Grey first. His burned skin glowed beneath two layers of salve. There wasn't much else she could offer—burns like that were a nasty sort. Keane had merely been toying with Grey. If he'd wanted him burned through, he could have done it in the blink of an eye.

Liana had lived many, many years, and that had only taught her the importance of exactly how swiftly it might happen. A high fey of Keane's power could break a man with one thought, which was why she'd had to resort to such underhanded tactics to get what she wanted. There were far more powerful fey afoot than she cared to tangle with. But she wasn't alone anymore, and she refused to let her prize head to court without her, no matter what he'd said.

"There." She pressed the last of the bandages into place. "Now, let's get to this."

Grey ignored her, continuing his explanation to the other man. "So Frey is with Veil, Steed and half the sentries are en route to what we assume is a plan to secure help from Junnie and her new Council, and we have until sundown tomorrow to make a deal with the fey."

"Rhys and Ruby?" the man asked.

Grey held the man's gaze but shook his head. No one, not even Liana's collection of feylings, had heard news of the two since the raid on the castle.

Liana pushed the man to standing. "As he says, we've not

much time." She glanced at Grey. "And what of Chevelle's plan?"

Grey shot her a look that told her he didn't appreciate her single-minded motivations. He was the fool, then, because Liana had far more than one incentive driving her.

"You'll hear it from his own mouth, if he deems you worthy to know."

Liana doubted Grey knew himself, despite the heated exchange the two men had shared earlier. Chevelle had a plan, though—she was certain of that. And he'd shown more confidence in his possible success in the last moments when she'd seen him than he had all along.

"I'll ready the horses," Grey told the other. It wasn't phrased as a question, but Liana recognized the pause afterward. He was waiting for confirmation that the other man planned to come along. She could tell there was no way he intended to stay, but she wasn't sure if it was for his brother or his duty to the crown.

It didn't matter to Liana. "None for me, thanks," she quipped. "Now, if we could just get going…"

Grey turned to snap a retort, but it was broken when a soft thud sounded on the long wooden table between them.

Liana froze. For a moment, she could only stare. Her words would not come to her. She could not form them to spell them to life.

She knew the key they needed, the diary of the high fey who had been Ruby's mother, was with the Summit boy. The halfling would never have entrusted it to anyone else. And yet there, among the herbs and potions on the scarred mahogany, lay a book marked with the same power signature that only one particular woman, powerful fire fey that she was, had carried.

"What shadowed sorcery is this?" Liana hissed.

Chevelle had thrown the book there, his mouth curving into what was nearly a smile as he watched her. He said, "It will suffice, then."

Liana began to reach for the book but drew her fingers back. "Is it spelled?"

He shook his head. "The mark is authentic. The rest, we'll have to leave to chance."

She forced her gaze from the book to stare at Chevelle. "How could it possibly be?" Everyone had seen the fire fey's death. Elven births were a spectacle, a celebration, and Ruby's mother had gone violently before them all as the venom of her babe sped to do its work. That part, at least, couldn't have been a ruse. Not only was the woman renowned, but her end had come by legendary means. She'd held a dark elf in her thrall and had brought into the world an impossible halfbreed child. Every detail had been told and retold, not only by fey, but by all kinds. She'd been gone for so long, and there was no fathomable way that book could have existed. But still…

"The mark is not from the fey your lore is so fond of," Chevelle answered, "but from another who also bears her mark."

Liana stared in bare shock. Ruby, a halfling who lived among the elves, who shunned her own kind in favor of unforested mountains and the rule of a crown… That she had the capacity to create the mark of a high fey so powerful… "That's not possible," Liana insisted.

Chevelle smirked and gestured toward the book, which was obvious evidence to the contrary.

"I refuse to be taken in by your trickery," Liana said. "This is more than ridiculous. She could not have hidden so much power."

Chevelle's long arms crossed over his thickly armored

chest as he straightened. "If that's so, then why do they want her so badly?"

"You know why," Liana snapped.

"And still you can't believe her capable of a simple mark?" He leaned forward again, pressing his palms onto the table where the book rested. "Or is it that you underestimated her? That she outwitted you by putting this second key into play before you even knew we'd need it?"

Anger boiled through Liana, but she caught herself before the room was destroyed. She needed them all for the time being, she reminded herself. She grabbed the leather-bound book from the table and flipped the pages open to reveal not the short, sharp marks of the fey, but loose elven scrawl.

THE ELDERS WERE a different story altogether. My father had given them orders to protect me and the child, and even though they followed through with them, they persisted in chattering about their concerns. The humans frightened them unreasonably. They constantly fretted, wanting to keep her, and me, from contaminating anyone else.

I attempted to reason with them, but they turned on me. "You don't understand. You never will! They will consume you. The humans will consume us all." Their hands shook as they spat out the words.

I didn't argue after that. I wouldn't have been allowed to leave the castle, anyway. Besides, it kept her from being paraded in front of so many visitors.

LIANA'S HAND came up to cover her mouth, returned to hover over the text, then turned another page.

. . .

MY FREYA HAS GROWN into a stubborn and willful child. She's prone to fits of screaming or crying. The emotion frightens the elders. It comes from her father, yes, but I can't see how it will harm her. The humans seemed to live their lives fine, controlling it well enough.

SHE WENT to turn the page again, but Chevelle snatched it away from her. Liana knew what was coming, though, as she knew the story by heart. There would be more humans. There would be a massacre.

She barked out a laugh, and the room went still. She scanned the faces of Freya's high guard, clearly unamused despite the utter thrill of it.

"Don't you see?" she asked them. "Your halfling fey has a stake in the game." She gestured toward the diary in Chevelle's hand. "When did she mark this? When did she know that this end would come?"

Chevelle remained silent. She could see his defiance and his doubt, but she also saw his hope. Even if they had only a decoy, they had created a chance. Their Ruby had created it for them.

Liana grinned. "Well, then, I accept this challenge. What is your plan, Vattier?"

2 2

FREY

V‍EIL LET ME STAND AT THE EDGE OF THAT CLEARING FOR A long, painful moment. I had to force myself to breathe, taking in every single sense of them. I had been near one, yes, but what was happening was something different. It hurt.

"You can feel them, can't you?" he asked.

He knew I could. He had to know. He had taken me there on purpose. I didn't know when Veil had moved, but suddenly, the weight of him was behind me, steadying instead of anything else it had ever been.

"Why?" I choked out. There were so many *humans*. "Why this?"

Veil placed a hand on my shoulder, careful of the metal bands that crossed my armor, the chains that tied the shoulder plate to broken strips of mail. "You know why," he answered. "Despite all Asher had planned, there was no keeping this secret from my kind." He meant the secret that I could reach into the mind of a human.

"It w-wasn't... I d-didn't—" My stomach turned at the image my mind had created from my mother's diary: throngs of them slaughtered for Asher at Council's hand. "I can't do this. Whatever it is, whatever you want—"

Veil's grasp on my shoulder tightened, and I knew the metal was starting to burn. "The fates," he reminded me. "This is your only chance."

My hands were shaking and slicked with sweat, unsure what to do. *Action*, my body told me. *Fight. Run.*

But Veil's amber eyes bore into mine, his grip holding me firmly in place. He was right. Even if he'd not prevented events from being maneuvered there, it was over for me. The end was coming for my Seven, and if I didn't play my cards right, the entire realm would be at the mercy of the worst of the fey. The power Asher had spelled into me could be stolen and used by one of them, by someone unable to restrain their worst instincts, incapable of any sort of control. My guard was separated, in the hands of a scheming changeling, a kidnapper with ill intent, and who knew who else. There was no one to stop it, no one to save us.

It was all because I'd followed my gut—my heart—instead of standing my ground. I'd forgotten what it meant to be Lord of the North. I had been perched on a precipice above a chasm of hopelessness, like my mother and hers before, and suddenly, Veil had pulled that small bit of earth from beneath my feet.

Humans. My thoughts taunted me. *Humans are right beyond that clearing.*

They brushed my mind. They were countless, endless, unceasing. "I have to get away from here," I told Veil. "Just for a moment, to clear my head."

"They are everywhere," Veil answered. "Beyond this band lie more and more. They've overrun the prairies and wood-lands. Our forests are next."

I shook my head. "I can't. Whatever it is—" Sick, twisted

imaginings began to claw at me. I didn't know what it was that Veil wanted or whether he wanted me to control and use them as my mother had. I could see the masses of them, mindlessly rising to swarm the fey court on my command, only to be slaughtered by the high-fey powers. It would be a sea of blood, borne of my own hands. I could not—*would* not—create an army of those beings as my mother had. I wondered if that was what he was after, to have them eradicated, removed from the land that even in that moment felt foreign to me, off in a way that didn't have to do with fey power or the presence of the creatures.

Veil knew me better than that. Regardless of our differences, even given the hopelessness of my situation, he surely knew me well enough to understand that it was out of the scope of my abilities and far beyond my will. I glanced over my shoulder, convinced we were absolutely alone.

On his own land, Veil was stronger than I was. With access to those powers, he could crush me in a matter of seconds. But in the new land, something was strange. He was vulnerable, and he was trusting me, trusting that I would listen and would not take that risk and try to end him before I ran beyond the trees and away from the entire mess.

It wasn't a true possibility, I supposed. I could not fathom leaving my guard or the realm. But it was something, because if he had wanted to convince me by threat or by bargain, all he would've had to do was let the heliotropes push against my will. He was letting me choose.

"All right," I finally told him. "I'm listening."

Veil turned to lead me away from this barrier of trees, farther into the brush, where we were insulated by distance.

There were too many of them. I only realized it when we'd walked far enough away. I'd heard the legends, the stories, but never had I imagined the scope of it. "How long?" I asked him. "How long have they been out there?"

Veil nodded, apparently pleased that I'd understood the gravity of the situation for everyone, though I couldn't be sure he knew I'd felt the unsettling change in the base power. "They've been encroaching on the boundary for some time now, but the problem has become widespread only recently."

Time meant something different to the fey, mattering little unless they awaited a prize. Years would slip by unnoticed, and then they wanted something, and suddenly seconds stretched with agony. Veil's words, his mention of my predecessor's plans, came back to me, and my heart lost its speed. "You said Asher." I peered at Veil, who'd lost a bit of his glimmering allure in the darkened copse. "How long did he know?"

Veil slipped the palm of one hand over the other. His wings were tucked tightly against his back. I didn't think he liked it there any more than I. "Nearly as long as the rest of us, I suppose."

"And this plan you mentioned?"

"Of course. His plan was to take control of them"—Veil's shoulder lifted, the movement too graceful to be considered a shrug—"by any means necessary."

My thoughts went again to the diary, to the history my mother had written. As a child, she'd lost her mother to grief, a mother whose brightness had been stolen from her after being bound to the Lord of the North. *By any means necessary.* I bit out, "Like stealing a light elf for his bride."

Veil smirked. "It wasn't the light magic he was after."

It was her gift, which had been the same as mine.

THEA

By all accounts, Junnie had relocated to the lands bordering the Northern territory. It had been an odd move, to say the least, putting her far away from her most dangerous adversaries and too close to the half-breed high lord she'd broken with Council over—or more precisely, the high lord who had broken Council with her.

Thea didn't have much love for the old Order of Light Elves and their politics, but no one was overly comfortable with destroying the one body who actually kept order among the Southern villages. Their laws might have been strict, their principles skewed, but they had maintained peace. Everyone knew what a Council tracker was—not much more than a bloodhound and murderer—and the threat of those men was enough to keep the more dangerous of the light elves from straying too far into the mountains. It had become hard to tell when one was safe and even harder to imagine when Junnie would finally get them settled into a new order.

"How much farther?" Steed asked. He'd been quiet for the better part of an hour, and Thea knew he was hurting. He did look improved, though, despite the sweat beading his pale brow.

She nodded toward a small rise ahead, the trees bright with midsummer growth. It wasn't midsummer, though, and few of the trees were native. "We should be getting nearer. A few lengths past that ridge, I'd wager." *Can't you see the signs?* she wanted to ask. She wouldn't risk it in front of the men, even if they did know he'd been poisoned by a fey blade, and even if there was no way he should have been alive, let alone sprinting down the countryside on horseback.

"No, not past the ridge," Steed answered. His horse, muscled and black with a long, even gait and narrow ears, came to a stop as Steed stared into the sparse trees lining the clearing beside them. "She's here."

Thea followed his gaze, finding a huge black wolf among the shadows, still as stone aside from its steady, measured breathing. "It's true, then? She has the gift as well."

Steed glanced at her over his shoulder, apparently caught off guard by the remark. Surely, he had to have known what the rumors said, that the power that allowed Lord Freya to join with the mind of a beast ran to her through this old line's veins. All of them were her ancestors, and all except two had been murdered at the hands of Lord Asher, before they'd taken their revenge on him, of course. A lot could be said about the Lord of the North, but half-human frailty or no, her enemies had a way of falling at her feet, and not in deference for her crown.

"Juniper Fountain," Thea called into the trees. "Steed Summit of the High Guard and One of Seven to Elfreda, Lord of the North, summons you to convene and confer upon the most urgent of matters."

Steed's brow rose.

"Make haste!" Thea yelled to the beast.

The wolf lay down in a bit of an unnatural manner then resumed a more wolf-like state. Its tongue lolled from its mouth, hanging between its sharp white teeth.

Thea leaned toward Steed. "What exactly does this magic do to them?" she whispered.

Steed shrugged. "I'm not entirely sure, but it never becomes less disconcerting."

Thea pressed her lips together. "So if she wasn't interested in talking and wanted just to roll my own horse right over me as I sat—"

"I could do it in a heartbeat."

The voice came from behind them, where all present had been watching the dark wolf among the opposite trees.

"Juniper," Steed said, apparently not at all surprised by the move and not interested in admonishing his troops for missing the woman's approach.

Thea frowned. She'd missed it as well.

"I've heard no sign of trouble," Junnie told Steed. "And yet you are here, upon some urgent matter and without another of your Seven."

Steed eyed the trees, though Thea didn't spot movement there apart from a gentle breeze.

"They are mine," Junnie answered. "You are free to speak here."

"The fey," he explained. "They've taken Ruby and set a trap, and they have Frey and the others beyond their borders."

Junnie clutched her robes. They were two shades of gold, with gilt leaves and fine ivy trailing the length of them and crossing over her hood. She threw them to the ground like so much trash, snapping her finger toward the trees. Several soldiers emerged from the copse behind her, dressed in dark tunics and pants, each armed with a bow and a sword. A thin male fetched her robes, folding them neatly as the others rushed past. The women wore no packs, simply quivers and sword sheaths, their robes no more than silk hoods and a single drape, their hair in tight, intricate braids. They were the runners, Thea realized. The men were their packhorses and a distraction to anyone who might see the new Council's procession when they traveled.

"I believe I have the key to get her back," Steed continued. "And she's left me a hint, some clue that led me to believe we might need you."

Junnie approached the horses, her gaze lingering on Steed's wan face. "You have me."

Steed clicked his tongue, and one of the spare horses from the rear of the pack rode forward. Junnie threw herself onto the animal's back without question, and Thea glanced at the others, who'd followed her from the trees. There were too many of them for the extra horses Steed had brought, so several dozen would have to run. But that was the way it was done in those armies—runners and scouts and forces spread across the terrain.

Thea's stomach plummeted. Their forces had suddenly doubled, and what had seemed like a harmless band of guards was turning into an army that intended to march right into the fey lands.

Junnie shouted directions at several of her men then turned back to Steed. "We have to make a stop."

Some unspoken message passed between the two. Despite Junnie having joined in Steed's dicey bid without blinking an eye, he didn't seem to like whatever the message entailed. He didn't argue, though, or press her at all. Instead, he inclined his head to give her the lead, and they went, dark and light elf alike, across the open clearing and through the solid line of trees that marked the edge of a Southern forest.

It was a winding, treacherous path, even as the trees ahead

parted, uncoiling from complicated braids and barriers where Junnie rode through. Thorns and hemlock brushed Thea's boots, tangled limbs snagging at her hair. The path became tighter, more snarled, and the late-day sun was lost to a canopy of leaves.

Eventually, Junnie slowed, giving some signal to Steed before dismounting. He threw up a hand, gesturing for the procession to wait.

Junnie walked farther into the trees, her steps careful and less swift. Her dark pants and tunic belonged there, blending seamlessly with the shadowy brush. She disappeared through a set of thick pines, barely rustling their boughs.

Thea waited, watching those pines, watching the men who watched those pines, and watching the trees with their chirps and chatter.

It was too hot. It smelled of freesia. It felt wrong, too alive. Thea wanted to throw off her cloak, but she couldn't tolerate the idea of her skin being uncovered in the closeness of those particular trees. She wanted to turn tail and run home.

Birds nested in the branches around them, and she couldn't help but feel like they were watching, all of them. She shuddered involuntarily, and Steed glanced at her sidelong. *Keep it together, Thea*, she admonished herself. *It's not the worst we're going to see.* It wasn't even close.

When Junnie finally emerged from the trees, she was in full fighting leathers, slim pants and high boots, a single knife sheath at her waist. Her form was lean. Her arms were covered not for heading north, but toward the deep, lush greens that were the colors of the fey forests. It wasn't that Thea had ever been there, but she'd heard it was warm and terrible and terrifying and all the things she never wanted to see. Even if Junnie didn't look eager, she'd apparently planned for that—a quiver full of pine and birchwood arrows rested on her back, each one tipped with polished steel.

Junnie latched a dark cloak into the clasps at her shoulders, glancing meaningfully at Steed before a shadowed form shifted in the brush behind her. For a moment, Thea thought it was the wolf, but the thing was too tall, its hair too long, its mouth less menacing and more a big, slobbery grin. It was a dog, she realized, a giant beast of a thing with black hair and mahogany eyes and nearer the size of a pony than any dog she'd ever seen. Its nose twitched as it took in all of them, the beast evidently satisfied they held no true threat as it panted, its ears lying loose on the sides of its massive head.

Thea was near speaking when the dog stiffened, its posture going abruptly from pet and possible plaything to guard and possible threat. It was only a moment before Thea realized why, and she did not miss that Junnie's posture had changed as well.

The whole of the group, already on edge, went silent and still as death when the next form shifted among the trees, stepping out between the two.

She was small and thin but not entirely fragile. "Scrawny with youth," Thea's father would have said. Her eyes were huge and bright beneath a mess of black hair, and her was face eerily familiar, down to the stubborn jut of her chin.

Thea could not believe what—who—she was looking at. "You can't be serious," she barked.

Steed turned his gaze from the girl to look at her, and though it wasn't the snap of the head that usually accompanied a reprimand, Thea knew she'd spoken out of turn.

She couldn't stop herself. "She is a *child*," Thea argued. "You cannot take her into the fey forests. Not among a *million* guards." She didn't need to gesture toward their army, which was far less than that sum.

The child was important. The child meant something to the light elves. Maybe Junnie had only saved her and the others had only allowed it because of their reverence for beasts—because there was a possibility the child carried that trait, the connection to animals that Freya and Junnie had, or some other, unknown talent that would be wrong to destroy. She had been picked by Asher among all the others who had not fared as well. But even if that were true, if she held that power and could connect with the beasts, it didn't matter.

The light elves wouldn't kill animals. The fey had no such compulsion.

But there was more, Thea thought, rumors of the girl's unnatural power. Whispers that she sought her own kind.

"The child won't stay here without me," Junnie answered. Her voice was even and cool. "I will not leave her. She remains at my side, or you fight this alone."

Steed ran a hand over his face.

"Because you care about her?" Thea said. She should really have strapped her mouth shut already, but she couldn't seem to get a rein on it. "How can you possibly—"

"Thea," Steed snapped.

She bit her tongue, hating the heat that ran through her. It was just a child—a small, helpless girl. If Junnie wanted her safe, the last place she should be was on fey lands.

Junnie stepped forward, gaze cutting sharply to the others among their guard. "The child stays with me. I will protect her at all cost." Her eyes stopped on Steed. "I will protect her as my own."

The promise was there, beneath her words. Junnie wouldn't simply protect the girl with her life.

She would protect Freya as well.

FREY

VEIL HADN'T SPOKEN A WORD OF THE HUMANS OR HIS PROPOSAL since we'd left the outer lands. I didn't know how many others knew what waited there or if they were aware of the danger. I wondered if superstition kept them from speaking of it or if it had been forbidden.

No, I thought, *something worse. Outright fear of what was to come.*

I hadn't given him an answer, but I was running out of time. It was little more than a day until the gathering, and I would have to choose. I'd thought Veil had the upper hand, but I'd been wrong. We were both at the mercy of the fates, and we would be lucky if either of us made it through with our lands intact, let alone our lives.

I had wanted to live in peace for so long, even though now my ideal peace comprised an entire kingdom, one that I'd spent my life trying to run away from. I had never wanted it, but looking back, it wasn't the throne I'd been running from. It had been Asher.

I'd finally gotten settled into my role, and the people of the

North were my responsibility. They were not to be bartered or risked. In the end, what Veil had offered hadn't been a true fey bargain. As far as fey trades went, it had been scarcely short of pleading. But I didn't know if I could give Veil what he thought the fey needed. I didn't know if he could deliver what he'd promised in return.

"The black one, you fool," Flora snapped.

Virtue glared at the other heliotrope. I didn't need their gift to know what she was thinking. Virtue was a fey warrior, not a maid and wardrober. But Veil wouldn't let anyone else touch me, only those two, who could feel any intent to harm that the other might do and warn him in advance.

"She is Lord of the North," Flora said over my head. "Black. Black. Black." She yanked on the braid she'd been twining with silver thread, and I grimaced, not only at the sting, but at the none-too-subtle imitation of a crown. It was ridiculous yet necessary and far too much like the banquets I'd been forced to attend as a child.

Virtue shoved a heap of black leather at me, unconcerned with me but paying close attention to Flora, who stood behind my back. "There. Black. My work here is done. I'll be patrolling the balcony."

"The screen," Flora ordered, gesturing vaguely in the direction of the opposite wall. They'd brought in a half-dozen trunks, all of which were open and heaped with fabric, ribbon, and jewels. Virtue might have been annoyed with attending me, but I knew she would soon be costumed as well. It was the high fey court on the eve of the fates' dance.

Virtue's head inclined toward Flora, but her glower only intensified. It was not just a reputation. The heliotrope was truly terrifying.

While Flora finished decorating my hair, Virtue stormed to the pile, jerked a folded screen free, and slammed it upright on the floor. She threw her companion what was either a salute I'd never seen or an offensive gesture that was nasty enough not to have been previously used in front of an elven lord.

"There," Flora said, patting the last braid into place. "Now change."

I drew the breath I would need to stand and cross the floor, because I wasn't sure I could put forth the effort to do both at once. It was bad enough at home with my own politics. The last thing I wanted to do was parade and pretend in some other land and in front of a mob anticipating my murder.

As I turned to step behind the screen, I caught sight of Veil across the room. He stood before the massive windows, overlooking his forests, still and silent and head of the fey high court for the time being, anyway.

He might have been watching those trees, considering what fates would come, but the sun glinted off the glass, throwing amber shadows against its surface and reflecting his gaze as it followed me.

I had become the hope for the fey lands, against my will and at my own peril. I couldn't blame him for it, but I would never forgive him. I would never forgive any of them.

I let my gaze stay leveled on Veil's reflection as I disappeared beyond the screen, and then I threw the pile of leather onto the floor, biting back a string of curses that would have made even a seasoned rogue blush.

Flora had removed my poultices during her ministrations, and the wounds had sealed to a handful of faint red lines. I thought my ribs might be bruised again, but the ache was background noise to the rest of my problems. The pendant Ruby had left for me was still tucked into the belt at my waist, so I slipped it over my neck to hide beneath the fey garb. I understood why they wanted her and what the stone in that pendant was meant to represent. What I didn't know was what Ruby wanted me to glean from the clue. I wondered if she thought we wouldn't follow her, whether she'd simply intended to leave us an answer about what the fey wanted, or if she'd thought I would not be fool enough to get caught in their first petty trap.

I tossed the filthy scraps of clothing I had left from the battle onto the tiled floor and slid into fine leather boots and pants. The slim shirt and vest fit me well, but the standard metal emblems of my line had been exchanged for carved leather, leaving nothing but black on black on black. It didn't feel strange, nothing unusual or out of place until I stepped free of the screen and found my reflection in the long wall mirror.

"Cursed fey," I told the image. The outfit was a nearly perfect replica of one I'd worn at a long-ago spring banquet as Asher's Second, a gathering I'd been unaware any fey had attended. I was therefore more than a little unsettled by the accuracy of every single detail. I glared at Veil's back, only to find that he'd changed his own ensemble as well.

If my wardrobe said *black*, his screamed *the sun*. He was resplendent in bronze. His chest, finally covered, was draped in silks embellished with ribbon and gems, and his crown was made of golden antlers, woven into a band and arching skyward in several sharp peaks. Long feathers were embroidered into his boot leather, golden ivy stitched into every seam. He smiled at my appraisal, apparently believing it was a courtesy—generous, even—to spread wide his amber wings. When he did, though, I couldn't help but be impressed at the spectacle in that room of mirrors and glass, even if I kept it hidden beneath an angry scowl. He was a true fey idol, as powerless as I was.

His words from the outer lands came back to me. *It does not matter how strong a king is if his court turns against him.* He was right, and it was time we took hold of the helm and steered the ship to storm and inferno.

"Fine," I told him. "We both look the fool. Now let us get on with your heathen ceremonies."

Veil frowned, which did nothing to diminish his regality. "Lord Freya. And we have been getting on so well."

"Save it for the gallery," I told him. "I don't have the energy for much more than that."

He ran a thumb over the ring on his third finger, a band set with a square-cut yellow stone. "Shall we get to it, then?"

I crossed the room, weaponless and bereft. Veil was my only ally there, and I trusted him only because he needed something from me. "Yes, let's."

It was an ugly, terrible game, and we both had our parts, our hidden cards, our final plays to make.

25

RUBY

"Even as we speak, the broken Seven make their way to these lands." Pitt's voice was smooth and impeccable, the rare ability to spell words to life made flawless by his immense power. He stood tall and regal, a king of ill intent if nothing else, his shock of light hair a contrast to the endless of black of his eyes. Ruby listened, contemplating the words he'd chosen and the information he'd left out, working on her plan. "They use their power to draw together armies, each of them fighting their perils to flock to the same destination, each of them ready to meet the same end."

She picked apart his clues, only arriving at assumptions that would do her no good. They were coming for her, but she'd known they would. Anvil must have split from the others, for no one else had the power to draw together armies. He would use his unusual gift to persuade them, that trait that caused strangers to immediately think well of him despite his stature and build. He would likely go to Camber, to gather those same fighters who'd stood by their side against Grand

Council. But they were dealing with the fey. She didn't know how many would truly join or how many could even survive.

And she couldn't know what other army he spoke of or which others of her Seven Pitt had meant. Ruby could only hope that Steed had followed her clues and that Freya and the others were together, despite what Pitt had said. She wanted to ask about Grey so badly she could taste it, but the words would have been like poison. She could never let on that he held her concern in that way, even if it had been spoken of again and again. She could not admit that weakness openly.

"And what of it?" Ruby asked. "Your interest lies in me. This has nothing to do with the Seven or the North."

Pitt smiled, the tip of his finger stopping just shy of his lips. "Ah, but it does. For, you see, the court holds your dear Elfreda. What is it you call her there—Lord of the North, ruler of your Kingdom of Dark Elves?" His eyes turned up at the edges, mirroring his sly smile. "This Freya is a prisoner of the fey lord of the sun, and her mate is at the hands of one of my own."

And just like that, the bottom fell out of Ruby's plan. Frey was separated from Chevelle, her anchor, who provided the only safe way to use her power. "You lie," she said. "Even as you bring those words from the black abyss, you turn them to suit your will. I will not strike a bargain with a fraud, a dirty spellcaster."

Pitt laughed, the sound echoing in the silent wood. The others watched in rapt attention, waiting for whatever end would come. It could be a swift execution, or possibly terms for a trade. Either way, the show would be brilliant, their patience a worthwhile exchange. "Well, I suppose I do incline them to my favor, but you are correct that my interest lies in you."

She bit down a curse. She'd cost herself knowing more, her

bad reaction keeping him from continuing his speech. She would have to pay for the other knowledge, give him something in return. "The bargain," she told him. "Let's have it. Name your price."

He *tsked* at her, shaking his head. "I'm afraid it will not be so simple, halfling."

Ruby's impatience began to show through, and he asked, "Have you somewhere else to be?" When she glared at him, he laughed again. It was his prize, the show in front of a growing band of fey. But he needed something from her, and she intended to be gone from that forest before the next moon.

"First," he told her, "a test."

Ruby's mouth went dry, though the thought of such a difficulty had already crossed her mind. She feigned as casual a response as possible. "On with it, then."

Pitt flashed his teeth, rising into the air. He watched her, waiting, and Ruby glared back, drawing her hands to rest on her hips. He knew she couldn't fly. Everyone knew she couldn't fly.

He bit his lip, his grin larger than ever, then snapped a finger at two of his men. They grabbed Ruby, one by each of her arms, and Pitt told them, "Careful, now. This one bites."

Ruby bared her own teeth, finally resigned to taking part in the show but bristling when no one approached Rhys beside her. "He comes with us," she told Pitt.

"Ah," he answered, "but if I didn't have something you wanted, then how would I keep you under control?"

Three guards did grab Rhys then, to restrain him. Ruby jerked an arm free of the spiders holding her only to be lifted from the ground swiftly. When they reached an unsafe height, she stopped fighting. They would drop her—she was certain. The keeper probably wouldn't let them kill her until he received his end of the bargain, but two broken legs would only make the trade that much easier, not to mention lessening her chance of escape.

She gave Rhys a promise with her stare. She would come back for him. She would do what she could, whatever she had to. He didn't look afraid, though, and she was sorry for that. A man of honor should understand the tangled disaster he was about to walk into.

There was a short, sharp call not unlike that of a bird, and the men at her arms took flight, sudden and reckless as they left her comrade alone in the heart of Hollow Forest. She would repay Pitt that feeling, the dread that tore at her insides. That would come later, though, because for the time being, she had a more pressing matter to resolve, a test at the hands of a dangerous changeling fey.

THEY FLEW FOR SOME DISTANCE, the forest thinning before eventually becoming rough patches of nearly barren land. The grass was low, yellowed, and worn, trodden by something other than fey. Ruby glanced at one of her captors and noticed that his dark eyes watched the sky, not the ground beneath them. It was as if he had no interest in where they were going, no stake in the game. She didn't believe that. The other held fast to her as well, the sharp thorn-like tattoos that traced the bones of their faces and arms the only decoration they wore.

Ruby had dispatched their brethren one by one as they'd fled with her from her castle home. She wouldn't mind doing that over again—maybe a measure less hurried, but more painful.

Pitt slowed, lowering toward a section of dirt that had been scattered with broken tree limbs. The spiders lowered as well, easing down to drop Ruby near the keeper. Their feet didn't touch earth, and Ruby readied herself to land softly when they let her go. They were overhead in a heartbeat, hovering just out of range—had she a whip.

Ruby's knees straightened, bringing her to stand facing Pitt across the same approximate distance—just out of range. That was when she realized the scattered limbs were not trees. They were bones. Dry, dirt-covered bones.

Dead fey didn't leave piles of bones. They grew quickly but rarely made it to old age. When they did, their skin began to lighten in color, thinning and separating from themselves like fragile husks to leave their exhausted bodies behind and return their magic to the earth.

She stepped forward, scenting something wrong. It was not a place where things came to die. It was a place where things were killed. It smelled of musk and must, of unfertile soil. The breeze brought in staleness and the faintest hint of smoke—but it wasn't that of a fey flame, she thought. It was harsher, that of a burning, long-dried oak. Ruby had tasted those scents before.

She stared at Pitt, who merely watched her take in the clues. "Not to worry," he said after a moment, "none of these nasty little creatures are near us here."

She knew what he didn't say: *not anymore*. "The test," Ruby told him.

Pitt rolled his head, stretching his neck and shoulders as if he was about to battle, despite the ease of his expression. He slid the tigerwood staff into its place on his back, the pale-blue stone that adorned the handle well within reach. Ruby's gaze followed as he gestured her past him, and she realized the bones continued into the grass. A line of them lay strewn through the field, spread out seemingly haphazardly but most definitely in a demarcation.

Pitt wanted her to cross that line.

That was the test—she could tell by his posture. But she couldn't see why. She walked forward slowly, lifting her eyes to scan ahead, where there were scattered, thin trees, not green enough and presenting too-narrow leaves. *Barren*, she thought. *This land is barren.* It wasn't the vegetation, nor the lack of beasts.

She edged up to the dotted line of bone, glancing once at Pitt. He watched her, expressionless and no less striking than the half dozen times she'd looked at him earlier. She did not know what would happen when she raised her foot to step again, but she did it anyway. She had no other choice.

Hollow was how the ground finally felt when her boot touched the earth. She walked farther though, because it was not an entirely uncomfortable sensation. She'd never liked the fey lands, with the roaring current of power beneath. It was a constant river of energy to the full-blooded fey, but to Ruby, it was only noise, a purl and a hiss that vibrated insistently and just out of reach.

She stopped, swallowing the laugh that bubbled up.

It was the test.

She smiled her most horrible grin and turned to Pitt. Since she was a child, she'd known they'd wanted her. It had teased the edges of her consciousness for the first few years, a quiet knowledge that she suspected had been gifted to her—maybe by her mother, but it was impossible to be sure. The children of the fey grew far faster than the elves, and soon, she had caught her older brother, Steed. They had come for her, then, playful and pestering, hinting that she would soon be theirs. Her brother had kept Ruby from the borderlands, knowing that to cross would have meant torment at best and a slow, painful demise at worst. But even when she'd strayed from Camber, far from the fey lands but outside of his watchful eye, the pixies and sprites tangled into Ruby's hair, whispering.

She had grown accustomed to such threats until a half-dozen seasons before, when the whispers had become frenzied. She hadn't known that was what they wanted. She had misunderstood. Fear had paralyzed them, though, driving them to neglect their own rules.

Think. Plan. Prepare ahead, she reminded herself.

Pitt, the keeper of silent things, was a fool.

She tossed her arms skyward, throwing her fingers open widely. Fire flew from her palms, devouring the scents and the air. Orange danced in red flares, flickering yellow and sparking to the ground. It ate at the dry grasses, clearing everything not flush with life. Ruby dropped her hands down and outward, letting it crawl throughout the field. She pushed the blaze harder than she'd done before, seeming to draw heat from the ground to her, seeming to feed the conflagration.

He was a stupid, arrogant fool.

Pitt studied her, evidently convinced she had more power than any halfling should be able to muster, and Ruby pushed harder. A blast of flame shot up around her, creating a wall of fire that arced at her back and sides. She made it dance, curl onto itself, and break like a wave crashing to the earth. The fire sucked back to nothing, suddenly choked of the power that had created it, and all that remained was the remembered heat and burned out field.

"This is what you wanted," Ruby said.

It was her test to see if her gift to use magic in the elven lands had been stolen from her there, drawn into that sieve, that newly hollow earth.

"Come," Pitt answered. "We have much to discuss."

Ruby crossed over the bones once more, feeling the slow return of that buried static. It was why he'd stayed beyond the barrier—to protect himself. And yet, he knew she wouldn't run. Her weakness in relation to the Seven was patent. It was going to cost her and probably end up costing one of them as well.

She'd made it past the test, though, which was in itself more than she'd expected. Ruby had never been able to draw on base power. The barren land meant nothing to her because the base power meant nothing. Pitt had been so focused on securing a remedy for himself that he had underestimated her. He'd been so determined to keep his bid a secret that he'd excluded others who might know she was more powerful than he'd expected—others who might have gathered precisely how her power worked.

She'd thought he had merely wanted the diary, but what she'd found suggested more. He'd wanted her, she realized, not for that secret alone, but so that he might have her bloodline in his hands.

Pitt's earlier words came back to her, suddenly and like a knife to the chest. They weren't holding Frey for an exchange as ransom for Ruby's diary. They wanted Frey. It was the only reason to take her second-in-command and why Pitt was holding Rhys at that very moment: to keep her in line.

Ruby had known that, as another half-blood, she would be important, but she'd misjudged the fey again. It wasn't that Frey could control the humans. It was merely that she'd been born and had lived.

There was a reason the crossing of blood was so disdained. Ruby recalled the woman in Asher's chamber, the human who, despite all possible tending, had died a horrible death. With Frey, things had been less complicated because her father had been human, but when it came to the fey, it didn't work so easily. Ruby's mother had found a way around it, a way for the magics to blend and for a half-elf, half-fey child to live. She had miscalculated, though, for no one expected the child to be venomous and to inadvertently poison her own mother.

Ruby's mother and Asher had been the only two who had successfully created half-breeds. Asher had done it more than once, but he had failed more than succeeded, and he and those children had been destroyed by both elves and fey. No one wanted to see the outcome of their survival, so all that remained were Ruby, Frey, and Asher's half-human child, Isa. Frey had told her that Junnie had chosen the name because the babe's human mother had died during delivery. The woman had been convinced the child would be a boy—a king, Asher had promised. Ruby couldn't help but note now that "king" didn't refer to any title in the elven lands.

"The bargain," Pitt said. Ruby snapped to attention, torn from her ruminations to stare at the changeling fey. They'd walked clear of the boneyard and closer to the dark-winged guards waiting low in the sky.

"Name your price," she answered.

"You," Pitt said simply.

"I would rather die."

Pitt nodded. "I might have settled for the book, but it is out of your possession, so you have nothing left to offer."

She wasn't sure how he knew it wasn't in her custody and could only hope it didn't mean he'd found Steed. She didn't flinch, though, playing on. "I do not need the pages. I had it memorized before my tenth season."

Pitt lowered a brow.

"*Power Studies and Magics, A Journal.* Page one: six tonics for the healing of a broken wing. Gather these ingredients outside of the dark night: six grain weight of freshly cut black horehound, the shed bark of an ironwood tree, three leaves of nightshade, the plumage of the summer wrentit, a gill of houndstooth oil, amaranth, and wormwood, a palm of poppy seed—"

"Enough." Pitt moved close enough that she could have

kissed his neck with a spiked metal tip, had she a whip. "While I trust you've had time to memorize it, you know I would not make the trade without seeing the fire fey's mark."

No one said her name aloud, not even Ruby.

"We make the trade," he continued, "when you secure the book from its place."

They didn't have Steed. Her brother was safe until he came after her, she supposed. She would buy time. She would do what she had to. Pitt was a fool. "She was more powerful than you," Ruby told him. "What makes you think you can pull off her magic and live?"

He smiled. "I'll have you."

26

STEED

Steed watched Junnie stare across the boundary to the wreckage and knew she'd been nothing but truthful. She hadn't known about the trap or the feys' plans. Trees lay scattered throughout the clearing, piled in heaps and sprinkled with ash. They appeared to have been uprooted, some tossed and others crushed then forgotten. A smear of black, something deadly enough not to have been washed away by weather, crossed the silted ground on the far side of the boundary.

Junnie's soldiers walked carefully across, stepping gingerly over stones and around bits of metal or cloth. One bent down, running a fingertip through the lightest bit of residue before bringing it up to sniff. "Spellcast," he said, glancing at the others, who stood farther through the clearing.

"Fey blood," called another from near a large ring of dark-red rocks. "And powders—some sort of protection spell, I'd wager."

They surveyed the area, glancing high and low, scenting

out fey traps as best they could. Steed turned to Junnie. "We don't have time for this, do we? Shouldn't we just chance it, cross, and see—"

Junnie looked at him then, and Steed's words cut short. She was worried, and not simply about Frey.

"What is it?" he asked.

"The boundary," Junnie told him. "It's been altered." She breathed deeply, glancing at the rocks beneath their feet. "More than that, I think. Stripped down to the barest of protection."

Steed stared at her. "I don't understand, how can you—"

Her look cut him off again. It wasn't fear that time, but a furtive glance at the girl, Isa.

Steed stepped beside Junnie and knelt, ostensibly examining the rock. But he watched the girl as well, seeing her pick up stones that should have been cemented to the earth, running small fingers through the moving water, catching bits of floating things before bringing them up to inspect in the morning sun. She shouldn't have been able to do that. "How?" he said.

"She is more human," Junnie answered. "There is less of our blood, and more of something… *other*."

Isa tossed a pebble into the deepest part of the stream, turning back to them, and Steed stood. Thea and their castle sentries were waiting on the grass before the boundary, unmoving as Junnie's trackers scanned the field. But no, they weren't trackers, Steed remembered. They were Junnie's warriors, trained not to search for those who opposed her, but to protect their new Council leader.

Steed's head still ached.

Junnie handed him a canteen. "On the far side of this ravine are some elderberries. I'll have a scout pick some up on our way through."

"Thank you," he told her. "But I believe I can make do."

She nodded. "I would imagine. Liana may be a changeling, but she'd never do more than temporary harm to someone who might increase her bargaining power."

Steed's brow drew down. He knew Thea and his men would not have told a light elf anything, regardless of whether she was a current ally. In any case, only a handful of them had been aware the changeling had been the one who'd ministered to him. She hadn't heard about Freya or Ruby, but she was aware of that. "How would you know that?"

Junnie shrugged. "It's been a long time coming, Summit. You fell into this mess just when it helped a…" Her voice trailed off, her head tilting toward the trees behind them as she listened. "The wolves," she finally said.

Steed turned with her to watch, waiting less time than he expected before Finn and Keaton burst through the low limbs and leapt over brush. They were fast, and they were graceful, even clearly exhausted as they were. A chill ran through Steed. Something was wrong. They were in a hurry, they were not with his Seven or Freya, and it appeared they were looking for Junnie.

Isa moved between Junnie and Steed, keeping near Junnie's back but not clinging to her. Steed could not tell if she was scared or had merely been taught to protect herself that way. He didn't think she was afraid and couldn't see a reason why she would be. They were wolves, the very creature Junnie had used to greet them in the forest. But beside Junnie, the girl looked so small, thin, and fragile, no more than a child.

But she was a child who could break through the ancient boundary, pulling stones from its path without notice. It had been altered, Junnie had said, stripped to the barest protection. The look on Junnie's face said there had been more to it than just the girl's ability—much more. The wolves signified that things were even more complicated than the mere issue with the boundary.

Steed glanced at his men, the sentries who knew these beasts as allies, and at Thea, new to her post and everything that entailed. She appeared uneasy at the wolves' arrival, but Steed supposed no more than those who knew how out of place it might have been to see Finn and Keaton running toward them, toward an ancient border put into place, when they had been men instead of wolves.

It could not be good.

The wolves raced on, leaping forward and bounding against one another through the grass and sand and stones to a hard stop before Junnie. Finn pulled up, pebbles sliding beneath his massive paws, his mouth agape and teeth on display as Keaton skidded on the grass then shook as if he'd been caught in the rain. But there was no dampness upon their fur, only bits of forest and twisted briars. They panted and whined, settling after moments to stare up at Junnie, intelligence and light in their wide wolf eyes.

She stared back at them, not speaking. Steed stepped forward. Isa moved farther behind her protector. He watched the strange lot of wolves and elves, and the *other* became more evident. The little girl was not reaching out to the wolves. She did not feel at ease or trust in her control of what might otherwise be wild beasts. They were not wild—they were ancients, only transformed into beasts after living past their age, but Isa was apparently not aware of that. She didn't watch them the way Frey and Junnie watched animals. She watched them cautiously and with a purpose, alert in the way Thea might have been. Living with Junnie, the girl would have been around animals enough to have grown accustomed, and yet she was having such a response. She could not connect with beasts. That was clear.

There was something else, too, something Steed hadn't entirely realized until he watched them together. There was a quietness about the girl that was at odds with her wide eyes and fly-away hair, something that felt hollower than the other half-breeds he'd known.

Thea shifted across the empty grass between them, and Steed glanced in her direction. He'd been watching the child, finally noticing these small things through the clearing haze of his treatments, but that was not where the sentries' focus was aimed. They were watching Junnie and the wolves.

His unease had been nipping at him, tugging here and there at things that were not quite right and should not have been happening, things that had nothing to do with the disappearance of his sister and the Lord of the North. But a new realization dawned, and it was no small concern.

Junnie could communicate with the wolves, not simply control them with the suggestion of movement and action and direction. She was *speaking* with them through her mind and *hearing* them speak back, which was something Freya had never done—it was something Freya had never known.

Steed waited, unsure for a moment if it would even matter. But he knew it would. It was another secret, another important piece of the puzzle withheld from Frey.

Junnie straightened, taking in a shallow gulp of air. She nodded, looked immediately to Steed. "We will have to restore the boundary, but that must wait. Keane and the changeling Pitt have taken Ruby. They also have possession of Rhys. And Freya is in the hands of fate." She glanced at the sky. "We need to go to her now, taking all the help we can get."

Steed's hands came out, palms up. He'd brought everyone he could. Castle sentries were all he had. There was no one else nearby, and the rest of his Seven had already moved into the fey lands.

"Not more men," she told him. The sun caught Junnie's pale-blond braids as she turned to scan the far trees. "More wolves."

27

FREY

THE HIGH FEY COURT IN SUNLIGHT WAS A DIFFERENT SORT OF beast. Magnificent flowers draped the newly-constructed dais, its birchwood frame painted in intricate patterns of gold and white. Light streamed into the clearing, catching on every size and color of blossom and every shape and shade of greenery. Wide, dew-covered leaves bordered a stair-step arena, where fey of all kind had gathered to watch. Each appeared in their own form of finery. Heavy jewels and a long sheer gown orna-mented a slender wood nymph, while fresh-moss waistcloths and snapped-twig headpieces adorned a pair of tiny timber pixies. A few of the more powerful fey dressed in armor, likely knowing they would be targets as the festivities progressed.

No matter the wardrobe, though, all wore their best gems, for the power would flow and ebb throughout the day until the fates' dance. There would be a change to the proceedings then, when a darker, more sinister energy would emanate from those same fey in a larger gathering.

We walked through it all to cross the court floor, Veil's

men clearing a great swath before us amid the crowd of fey. The multitude was of all shapes and sizes, but I could not help but feel small. There were so many, more and more with each breath.

My steps were steady on the flat stone pathway, my eyes directed straight ahead. Chatter rose and swelled, breaking off as we passed and fey bowed, nodded, or simply stood staring. That was the way of the fey court—each kind had their own rituals and their own laws, even if one cause did unite them. I followed at Veil's back, the high fey lord's costume seeming grander still in the gathering of creatures. Their deference to his presence was a clear sign of just how powerful he was.

Veil was strong, and he held sway among each of them. He'd been head of the court since I was a child. I wouldn't think about what had happened to his predecessor.

We passed in front of the stone sculptures, each reaching skyward with the sun upon their would-be faces. They did not seem to be creatures in the light of day, only indistinguishable forms. It was the shadows that transformed them, making them appear as the terrifying objects they truly were.

The crowd grew restless as we approached the dais, the power humming through them stirring the barely-under-control energy within me. I had to work constantly to contain it, to keep it from boiling up with the instinct to lash out. It was meant to protect me, to help me get away. It knew what was to come, and it wanted out of that as badly as I did. *Now*, it said.

A water sprite rolled through the air, screeching in a hawk's cry before suddenly dipping into the space between the sculpted figures and the walkway that had been cleared for Veil. A shot of power came from one of the shadow stalkers, so strong that it resonated all the way back to me, overpowering the other sense of it, the feel of it swimming around me. I watched as the magic connected with its target—it didn't merely toss the thing back, as I'd expected, but completely obliterated the fey's slight form. The crowd exploded into cheers. The ceremonies had officially begun.

I held myself perfectly still except for my even stride. Veil had not missed a beat, and neither would I. We would maintain some semblance of control, if nothing else.

Veil sidestepped the remnants of the water sprite's clothes, the fey lord's silken wardrobe swaying against drawn-back wings. He paused at the first step onto the platform, holding a palm up for me to take as we ascended the short set of stairs. It was not because I was in danger of tripping. It was for the gratification of his audience.

It was the show.

I lay my fingers on his palm, each of us placing a boot to step in tandem. When we reached the platform, Veil turned us both, keeping my hand over his as we stood before a row of seats. The center chair was throne-like, but only in that it held status above the others with its height and grandeur. A massive gnarled root system rose well above Veil's back, braided and woven into patterns within patterns. Beside it was a low, wide bench of antler and birch, and behind me were two thin chairs of alder and yew. I didn't question which I had been assigned to, because on top of the chair to Veil's left was a spiked, slaughtered bird. Its feathers had been spread wide, its wings decorated with dark, sandy pebbles and blackened string. A soft blue ribbon wove through its feathers, curling gently below its head and beak to keep them in view, so everyone could clearly see the jewels set into those dead eyes.

I had to remember that. *This is not home. These are not*

remotely the politics I am accustomed to, not the rules we all rely on. Beneath this current of power lies something sinister, itching to be freed.

"My people," Veil said to the crowd, startling me into the moment to see him raise a hand. "We gather today in preparation of a great tradition, one created before the dawn of our kingdom, one put into place to satisfy the boundless forest, our earth, and the sky. I call to you, join me, and let us pay the fates their blood so that their spirits may dance!"

Veil's wings burst open full sweep, stretching behind us all and leaving nothing visible to the crowd but the top tip of his throne. It became a gilded crown of sorts, floating above his golden head. In that moment, he was more magnificent than the sun, and I held tightly to the power within me for what would happen next.

I had felt great power before, but the earth didn't tremble as it had when I used the ability Asher had gifted me—stones did not rattle, and soil did not break. Instead, what I felt was a slow, burning sort of buildup that swam and swelled beneath us until it rose to swallow my very breath.

It was Veil's gift, and it was strong enough to change the seasons.

He harnessed the base energy, directing it up and through his own form. I did not know how he could possibly contain it and remain whole, given that even standing so near created a suffocating pressure in me that threatened to crush us all. Veil pushed it outward, blasting the energy above the rapt onlookers and into the atmosphere. The power that had been crushing me became biting hornets, the sting of ice, and the thrill of adrenaline all at once. It took to the sky, radiating heat and light and exploding into bursts of brightness that crackled and sparked, trailing smoke and embers in its path.

It was only a fraction of what he was capable of, and the

crowd took it in for one silent moment before Veil dropped his hands. Spikes of power and fragments of the explosion shot through us all, and I barely kept my feet. Veil smiled at the crowd.

The roar of applause was deafening.

28

CHEVELLE

THE PLAN HAD BEEN TO SEAL THE BARGAIN AT THE BOUNDARY between lands. Given that the marked volume was in fact a ruse, there was no other way to protect it from being discovered. Chevelle had toyed with Liana's idea to rewrite the pages of the diary into a fey journal, to make a clever forgery that would take longer to detect as a fake. But they didn't have the time, and he couldn't exactly trust her with the contents of the diary, even if they had to trust her with their lives.

She'd sent word ahead, requesting to meet with Keane and two other high fey. Chevelle wasn't certain which of them had taken Ruby or whose custody she might currently be in, but he doubted Veil had been directly involved in her capture. Chevelle would never have been able to draw the high fey lord from his duty during the ceremonies in any case, but Veil had taken Frey at the fey trap on the boundary, had stepped in to remove her from a situation that could only have benefitted his kind if it had been allowed to play out.

It would have benefitted Keane more than the others, perhaps, and it was openly known that Keane was Veil's greatest adversary at the moment. The fire fey had been working to turn court against its current high lord, and by all accounts it was succeeding in the outer regions. The entire situation might have been enough to cause Chevelle hesitation, but he knew how fey politics worked. Someone devious had Ruby, and it was either Keane or one of the others Liana had called on. Veil was not a true participant in the game—Chevelle knew he had spared Frey.

That didn't mean Chevelle had to like it.

"Get your head in the game, Vattier," Liana told him.

He didn't spare her a glance. Anvil and Rider had gone to gather men, taking a direct route south of himself, his band of sentries, Liana, and a poorly-healed Grey. "Span out," he commanded, scanning the field that stretched before them. The men did so without question.

They'd been in a full run from the castle until they reached the low blades of grass marking the protected ground that brought them to the boundary. Chevelle was glad, for once, that they had someone fey with them. Liana would be able to feel the bindings the ancients had laid in place. Something had gone wrong before, some fey trickery or broken magic that had allowed the lot of them to be trapped by Keane and the others.

He didn't know how they'd managed it, but it wouldn't happen again.

"Go ahead," he told her. "Find us a route, and we will follow."

Liana narrowed her gaze on him, her eyes going white before ghosting to steel gray. She preferred that color for battle, and it was no secret that she was ready to play. "The entire boundary line has a fault. There are components here I have no control over, circumstances beyond my not-so-meager limitations." She glared across the open field. "This will need to be resolved, but it will not be done before the fates dance."

"Enough with the riddles," Grey said. "Where do we cross?"

Liana managed to look annoyed, despite having expended all that effort into her battle face. "It isn't my fault your mind is incapable of seeing the truth in simple words."

Chevelle stared at her.

They waited.

"Fine," she huffed. "Follow eight beats behind me." She pointed at the sentries. "And keep them on this side until the trade."

She strode toward the barrier, her feet soundless on the bed of rock, and Chevelle counted to eight before starting behind her. Her steps did not splash into the running water, finding purchase instead on small bits of sand and silt as her magic parted the flow momentarily with each stride.

It should have been impossible, even for a changeling.

Chevelle kept his gaze on Liana when a shadow shifted among what was left of the fallen trees. Freya had destroyed so much of it. The power within her had torn free more strongly than she intended and faster than she could have realized on a good day—nothing in range stood a chance when she was angry, and she had been distracted, angry, and trapped.

The landscape went silent, suddenly void even of the rustle of leaves, and all present took notice. Liana's boots came to rest on the fey side of the ancient earthen barrier. "Show yourselves now," she told the debris-strewn landscape. "We have no time for folly." One hand rose toward the clouded sky. "Not with the fates' dance upon us."

The clearing was eerily still. Chevelle had wondered at it before—the fey were not exactly friend to the wildlife, but he wasn't certain how they'd managed to keep the forest devoid of fauna altogether. He knew why: Frey. They understood what she could do with beasts and the way she used them to subvert magic and spellcasting, to break through protected boundaries. He glanced at the ground beneath their feet then dismounted. "Liana," he started.

She put a hand into the air to still him without looking back. Her shoulders were tense, her ears tilted toward a sound he could not hear. "We have the key," she told their surroundings. "The prize one might steal a halfling or an elven lord for."

Grey's horse nickered.

"We will not cross this boundary," Chevelle said to whoever might be listening. "The trade happens here."

The sky flickered. It was not a flash of lightning nor a glint of sun. It was something else, something unsettling that put pressure on his chest and caused an ill feeling to grow in the pit of his gut.

"The ceremony," a voice said from the other side of the rock bed, "has begun."

Chevelle was sure that the figure had not been there moments before. It was a changeling, one he was not familiar with—though with a changeling fey, it was difficult to be sure.

Liana took a step back, positioning her body to face the thing. It was not a friend, despite the manner with which it spoke. He wondered if it was taunting them, reminding them that the flicker had been Veil's power, that it could be felt even there, and that on his own land, nothing was out of the fey lord's reach. Or maybe the creature had come to get away from such danger, keeping its distance from the court ceremonies for precisely that reason. *No*, he thought.

Liana turned to Chevelle, letting the undiluted fear show on her face—her *true* face. "Run," she said, but it was too late. Winged beings had burst into the atmosphere suddenly, entirely engulfing them with darkness and rapid wingbeats and a stench that could only mean one thing: spells.

Chevelle reached for his pocket, the black beasts biting and clawing at every inch of exposed skin. He grappled for the pouches, unable to see, hear, or sense anything but the spikes of wings and dark chaos. He reached a leather binding and pulled, not knowing if it would be the right concoction to help. Powder spilled across his fingers, burning and bubbling when it mixed with his blood. It was the madness of an uncontrollable fire blast, the stinging beasts' attack like being blinded in a midnight hailstorm. He could do no more than breathe and grasp for more of the concoctions tucked away in his vest.

One felt spongy, tied together with string, and the bird things ripped at it, knocking the package free of his ragged hand. He reached for his waist, drawing a spelled blade up and through the cloud, but there were more and more, and nothing could keep them at bay. Words came to him, ancient and powerful and just as useless as everything else. Two more pouches were in his bloody palm, and he cut through again to meet hand-to-hand. He sliced both packets open, throwing their powders together into the cloud. The mass of things screamed and sizzled then returned to him tenfold to bite and sting.

He screamed more spells, drawing the last of his potions from a pocket near his belt. It was the strangest, the most foreign of mixes he'd found among the castle's supply. And it did nothing.

Not nothing, he realized, for the air was sweet, and his ears began to ring. He cursed. Heat rose from his feet, burning within his boots and higher, scorching flesh and cloth alike. He didn't know if it was real, if the powder was consuming him or—a high-pitched squall cut through the ringing in his ears, a light like the sun searing through the blackness from earth to sky, parting the spelled beasts, splitting their wings to fall in feathered bits that floated ceaselessly to the ground.

The birds were gone, the air was clear, and Grey was nowhere to be seen.

29

FREY

T̲ʜᴇ ꜰᴇꜱᴛɪᴠɪᴛɪᴇꜱ ʜᴀᴅ ᴄᴀʀʀɪᴇᴅ ᴏɴ ᴛʜʀᴏᴜɢʜᴏᴜᴛ ᴛʜᴇ ɴɪɢʜᴛ ᴀɴᴅ into the second day. The sun rising over Veil and his court on the dawn of the fates' dance was the most stunning thing I'd ever witnessed, and it had done nothing to prevent my stomach from being braided into knots. The dread of the coming night was worse with every instant that passed with the brutal fey. I knew my Seven would be arriving and that they would reach us eventually, in the light of day. Veil had called the fates to decide my bid against Keane, and Keane's against me, but it was bigger than that, and each of us knew it. No one would miss what would take place at nightfall.

But when the first of my guard did arrive, I had to still myself. I fought the need to call out, to go to her.

It was Ruby, bruised and dirty, her hair a tangled mess. But she was alive. *Ruby*. A tall changeling fey walked beside her, his skin ablush with spring. The men who followed had Ruby tied with braided hemp, three of them holding tightly to the rope ends. *Spellwoven, then*, I thought, and I wanted to punish him for the offense. She was not his prisoner. She had been stolen from my home.

I stood. I shouldn't have stood, but I did. It was too late to change that, too late to do anything differently for any of us.

Pitt continued his entrance, smiling and nodding at the attending fey. He wasn't unaware of me—he was working to offend. He planned to keep Ruby, and an outburst by me could only help him secure his prize. The best result for Pitt would be my premature death. I stared at the pompous beast.

He wore plain clothes, a pale robe that masked his slender frame, and a woven-ivy cuff upon his wrist. His feet were bare and unnaturally clean, and his right hand held a jeweled ivory staff tipped with the largest crimson stone I'd ever seen. *A ruby.*

My eyes shot to Ruby, recognition plain, but her gaze remained straight ahead. The stone was *my* ruby, the one I'd taken from my family vault in the village so long ago, the one Chevelle had traded to Ruby in her Camber home before I had ever been restored to the throne. The whole thing was too deep. It went too far back. The fey had seasons upon seasons to plan their attack, and I was incapable of catching up.

I was blind, unable to stop it. I could not use my magic there—I could not risk leaving it to their kind. I was bound, again and again.

Veil touched my hand, and the gesture brought my awareness to the heat there. I glanced at him where he sat beside me. He did not need to warn me that I shouldn't lose my temper. I knew that. But it was a reminder of how deeply we'd been thrown in this mess. "For Ruby," I told him.

And that quickly, the deal was done. With just those words, I would keep the humans at bay, whatever the strange sorcery was that subdued the base magic within their range, and Veil would enter the fight for me to secure Ruby and get us all out of that mess.

I turned back to the audience to see speculation bright in the eyes of those who'd been near enough to hear. They did not matter to me. "Pitt," I said across the crowd, "you hold an elven high guard, one of my Seven, by means that are beneath you. I suggest you release her now."

Pitt continued his slow walk toward the dais, his false beauty on full display as he nodded to those who acknowledged him. When he did eventually look at me, it was plain that he felt that the only thing beneath him was that particular elven lord, me. "The halfling was gifted to me, which by fey law makes her mine by right."

"She was stolen," I told him. "I will have her back, or you will pay the consequence."

Pitt shrugged. "You cannot harness the base energy. There is no one here who would fight in your name, no one who stands a chance—"

Veil rose to his feet beside me, the sweep of his wings barely brushing my back. He would touch me then, there in his court and among those spectators, with my wardrobe stripped to leather, unable to burn him. He said, "I stand for Elfreda, Lord of the North and the Kingdom of Dark Elves."

The atmosphere went silent. Pitt stared. It was clear that no one, not even those who had been spreading rumor of the high fey lord consorting with elves, had expected him to toss his bid into the ring.

"Certainly," Pitt said to Veil, "you do not intend to take such risk over a paltry crossbreed?"

I let that one go. Everyone could assume it had been a reference to my guard.

Veil looked back at Pitt and said evenly, "I do."

The crowd erupted into laughter and cheering, pockets of

them already placing bets on the night's newest event. It was the biggest show in eons, featuring not only the fate of an elven lord, but Pitt, the mightiest changeling who'd ever fought in the high court, against the court's current leader, who was undoubtedly the most powerful fey present.

I took a breath, tightening my trembling hands. Veil was formidable, no small adversary. But it was Pitt, who'd been dubbed a stonemaker, the keeper of the stones. I didn't look at the forms on the court floor. I'd seen them all before. Half, maybe more, belonged to the changeling fey. He had won them in his battles, his power overtaking every opponent he had ever come against in challenge. If Veil lost, come sunrise the next day, he could be frozen there, no more than eternal stone, and he wouldn't have been the only one.

I hoped it was Pitt who was turned to stone. More than anything I'd ever wanted, I needed it to work. I had made a deal with the fey.

Ruby finally glanced at me, her eyes rolling down to the chain that pressed against my neck. Both of us knew what rested beneath the leather at my chest—the pendant, her clue. Ruby shook her head, clearly annoyed. I stared back at her unapologetically. If the clue was meant to be so effortlessly resolved, she'd clearly left me the wrong one.

Veil threw his hands into the air, gesturing grandly to the riotous crowd. "Let the festivities resume!"

They hadn't needed his permission. The groups of fey exchanging stones and bets widened and split, a chain reaction rushing through the assembly. Fights and cheers broke out at random, the base power thrumming with each small battle, feeding on energy it hadn't rightfully won.

The creatures were not meant to die. The fey had found the connection, fed it, and created a ceremony of celebration and blood. They were stealing lives to feed the base power, and it was sickening.

Pitt climbed the low steps flanking the dais and took a seat among the highest of high fey, leaving Ruby tethered, rope enough to stand on the open stone floor, level with the changeling's feet.

My jaw twitched with a suppressed growl.

"Your halfling looks well," Veil noted beside me. His tone was conversational, the complete lack of concern for what he'd agreed to almost entirely believable.

"I would wager a lesser being would not have fared so well," I answered not quite as convincingly.

He smiled. "You know I do love a wager."

I glared at him. Several among our audience snickered. Someone screeched in the arena, and fey surged toward the noise and back again. The mass fell silent, the power ebbed, and then they cheered as it returned stronger than before. My skin sang with it in a tingling, stinging rush that made me want to double over and heave across the finely polished steps. *Let us pay the fates their blood.* Veil's words would stay with me if I made it out of there alive, and I hated them all for it.

The sun was lowering in the sky, throwing color across the spectrum of fey. When the throng moved again, the dark, sharp figure of Keane became visible. He moved like a panther, swiftly and cleanly, at odds with the nightmare of his form. He had a mob, I could see—a large group of dark-clad spiders formed up to walk in rows. Keane made his way into the arena, letting the other fey disperse as he watched me with a grin. I could taste the bile. I hated that place. My magic wanted to end him. It wanted so badly to be set free.

The spiders split, their tattooed faces impassive as they displayed their prisoners. *No,* my mind screamed at the sight of those prisoners, but I held the word in check. Something worse was about to happen.

Fire exploded at the steps of the dais, Ruby's spellwoven ropes fighting everything she threw at them. I had seen Ruby angry, and I knew what her power could do, but they had prepared for her outburst. They had wanted her to show her strength in front of every fey. It made her a bigger prize.

I pressed my lips together, unable to intervene. My bargain had been made. Veil had agreed to fight for Ruby, and I had taken on Keane, but Pitt's men arriving with Keane was worse. Such cooperation between two high fey was competition—an actual, verifiable threat—for Veil.

In the center of those men stood Rhys and Grey. Keane preened, shifting to afford Ruby a better view. Rhys was bedraggled and beaten, but it appeared he would live. Grey, though—*oh, Grey*. I thought I would be sick, but Veil's power brushed me again, changed from stinging to heat, to the rays of a noonday sun. It didn't burn me. The burning had been all Grey and Ruby. Ruby was fire brought to life.

"I will end you," she promised. "You will scream and beg my name."

Keane tittered. It was especially unpleasant.

Liana must have ministered to Grey, for his skin was oiled to a sheen, but the damage was unmistakable. He would be scarred, even if Ruby had a chance to help him by the light of tomorrow's dawn.

Veil's heat subsided, and I was unsure if it had truly been meant to settle me, or if it was his penned anger, boiling within as my own did. He had made a deal to save his realm, but it appeared that he would also be risking his position at court. He'd pledged to fight on behalf of an elven lord, a halfling, and those two fey were working together, which could only mean they intended to displace him.

But I didn't know which one intended to do so.

Pitt, obviously, was the most powerful, but he was a changeling, and changelings didn't serve as fey lords. So the question of what Keane had promised the other remained.

My gaze traveled to Ruby, to Grey, to the tremble in my own hands. It stayed there, seeing the grip tightened into itself, nearly drawing blood at the very idea.

A pixie flitted in above the chaos, landing on the shoulder of one of Veil's men. He listened, flicking the tiny thing away once it had said its piece, then signaled to Virtue. She swooped in, listening to the news with an intensity I'd seen only among her kind. She wore her best fey armor, deep lavender to complement her skin, and an array of thin wooden spikes at her belt. She had come to kill, just like the rest of them, but she had a job to perform first.

She moved quickly from the man to Veil's side and spoke quietly into his ear.

When she departed, returning to the air as sentinel, Veil looked displeased. I waited, wondering how hard it might have been for his heliotropes to be around an assembly so large and if it would hurt them the way the mass of humans affected me. I considered whether that was why they preferred to fly just out of range, away from the thrum of anticipation. Eventually, he said, "Why must you make everything so difficult?"

"Yes," I answered, "this was all because of me."

His wing twitched irritably. He rose and addressed the crowd. "Joining us for tonight's festivities, upon my invitation." Veil gestured toward the trees, thick foliage being blocked by a thicker crowd. My stomach dipped. *What else?*

I watched the fey parting effortlessly and was alarmed to see Anvil leading a pack of men from those trees and onto the stone court floor. I scanned the newcomers, recognizing a few of them as Camber men as more and more followed behind. Rider came then, wounded but seemingly able, ahead of the largest band of rogues I'd seen in ages. They were dressed in battle gear, paint upon their chests and faces, hammers and spikes in hand. They too were killers, their methods nearly as brutal and violent as the feys'.

Veil glanced at me sidelong. I gave a small, one-shouldered shrug. I stared at my high guard, willing them to produce Chevelle from somewhere behind all the mess. Anvil's empty gaze stared back at me with no promises in his eyes, barring his vow. He'd pledged fealty to me when I'd been a mere child, and it was as strong as ever. I nodded gratefully, hoping he could not see the truth of my distress.

I needed more than vows. I needed my Second.

Chevelle finally did show up in the middle of the mayhem before a setting sun. Six high fey faced off, spears and horns and sharpened bones spraying blood as far as the center stones. The court was alight, excitement and power vibrating through every single being present, with fevered dancing and wanton screeching piercing, along with the occasional torturous scream. My nerves had been overworked, the constant tension fatiguing my muscles as well as my mind. I'd expected his appearance to be a reprieve.

I should have known better.

30

CHEVELLE

CHEVELLE HELD UP THE DIARY, FULLY AWARE THAT IT COULD GET him killed. They'd come too late, the attack at the boundary slowing them just enough to force his hand, and he would have to play through the dangerous ruse, to risk the fey finding out before they'd had a chance to get safely out of the fey lands.

Liana sang, some wild bird call that trilled higher than nature ever intended, and parts of the crowd settled down, turning to see what new thrill might await their frenzied delights. Fights had broken out in the packed arena, where pockets of drinking and betting and blood abounded. One particularly gruesome battle was near its end, and Liana and Chevelle picked that moment for their entrance.

They had the audience's attention. Enough of the crowd was watching that he should have begun his offer of trade. But Chevelle was frozen, unaware that time was passing, even if it was time they desperately needed to use.

Freya sat high upon the court dais, practically mounted on the stage as an ornament for the high fey lord. Veil watched him from his golden throne, but Chevelle had no interest in returning the stare. He could only see Frey, her armor gone and slick black leather covering her from neck to toe. Her dark-green eyes were lined in charcoal and filled with pain and exhaustion. Braids adorned her head, threaded through with ornaments, a makeshift crown. There was tension in her body, and he suspected she was having a hard time holding back her power in the current of madness. He could feel it swimming through the masses, and it was affecting even him. But there was something else, some warning in her gaze.

Liana nudged him. He glanced at her and hesitated. She threw up her arms.

"I have brought a lovely gift," she told the audience. She smiled graciously at the crowd, pausing pointedly when her attention landed on Keane and Pitt.

Ruby, he thought, shocked to see her there alive. She was tied in charred bands of braided hemp, her anger boiling below the surface as she stood at the feet of the platform's steps.

"He has a trade," Liana offered. She gestured toward the book in Chevelle's upturned hand. "And it is that for which you fools have yearned for many, many years." She bowed, spinning closer to the dais and letting her form shift-to-and fro. It made Chevelle's stomach turn.

She came to rest a few lengths from Ruby, keeping Chevelle and Frey in her line of sight. She'd solidified and chosen a color—the entire display had been a ploy. She'd merely wanted the crowd settled and cleared from a decently sized area, and it had worked beautifully. On the night of the fates' dance, one gave a changeling her space.

Liana looked up at Pitt, though her smirk was more likely aimed at Keane. "Opening bids?"

Keane hissed, but neither changeling gave notice. Interested, Pitt asked, "Terms?"

"The halfling, of course."

Pitt flicked a finger, indicating that Chevelle should bring the diary closer. It was too much of a command, an offhand gesture he might use with his servants. Chevelle moved anyway. The sun was sliding lower, throwing red and purple and orange against a thousand stones and shards of glass. The reflections of it caught the statues, wet with blood and reaching toward that dying sky.

The fates would dance in a matter of minutes. They had no time.

He gave himself distance between Liana and the others, holding the diary close to his chest, the fire fey's mark plain to those who would know it.

Pitt twitched, not entirely a tell, but enough on a changeling's face to give away shock. He'd not expected such a proposal, not from Chevelle and certainly not from Liana. He opened his hands toward the two and gave a small shrug. He didn't truly need Ruby. He only needed her knowledge. "It matters not whether the secret is in blood or ink. I shall trade the book for the halfling."

One of Pitt's men tugged on Ruby's rope, jerking her toward the stairs. Chevelle started to open his mouth to speak, to add his terms before the bargain was sealed. It must occur after the fates' dance. The trade must be made when they had time to run, to get to the border before Pitt had opened the record to find it was not his fire fey's potions, but an elven girl's diary.

He never got the chance.

"No!" Frey shouted. "There is no bargain to be made among my guard on my behalf. I have spoken for Ruby. The high fey lord will fight."

The entire arena went still. Chevelle turned to Freya, staring first at her form, solid and strong and standing atop the court dais, a feathered sculpture appearing to sprout wings at her shoulders from the top of a throne. When he looked to Veil, Chevelle saw his own shock mirrored, doubled, circling quickly to something dark.

Fury.

Spikes of sunlight shot through the sky, lightness disappearing below a purple horizon. The sun was setting, but Veil's heat could be felt through the entirety of the clearing. Frey's words echoed again and again, spiraling down until Chevelle could come to only one conclusion.

She'd made a deal with the fey.

FREY

THE HEAT OF SUMMER WAS BEHIND ME, VEIL A BURNING EMBER on the hottest day as he sat upon his golden throne. I'd betrayed him. My Second had shown up to save me, to give the diary to the changeling and retrieve Ruby so we might walk away before the fates' dance, and I had refused. I had forced Veil to remain in the fight even though he was at a disadvantage with his own kind, not simply because of the encroaching humans, but from a coup—with apparent players from both the fire fey, the changelings, and it-was-impossible-to-know-who else. Veil had given us a lifeline with the bargain, and I'd agreed because I'd had no other choice. But Chevelle had shown up, offering to save both me and the fey lord from this challenge, and I'd refused. In front of everyone.

It was the safest bet. It gave us the best chance.

The sky was turning, nightfall was upon us, and the half-breed elven lord had betrayed the highest fey. I cleared my throat. "We all know why the changeling wants Ruby. The gift she holds is her namesake, her mother having known that she was not tethered to the base power as the rest of you." Rubies were one of the few stones that could hold power outside the fey lands. I stepped forward, making my voice louder and my intentions clear. "You will not have her."

Veil rose to stand behind me. I could not see him, but I felt the heat and could see his movement register on the stunned faces of the fey below.

"I will protect your kind from the draw on your power. I will stave off that drain and keep the humans at bay." I inclined my head toward Pitt. "But only if I don't stand in tomorrow's dawn as eternal stone."

Pitt grinned wickedly. He understood that I hadn't trusted him to uphold his end of the bargain. I knew my Seven and I would never make it out of there alive. I needed him dead, and I would let Veil do it before attempting myself.

Nothing could have made the changeling happier.

"Then I propose a separate bargain," announced Chevelle. He glanced first at Keane and then Pitt, keeping the table open to whomever held the cards. "The diary for the others, Grey and Rhys. Without challenge, a simple bargain alone."

Pitt turned to Keane, making it clear that Grey and Rhys were under the other man's control, which meant that either Keane's men had captured them, or they'd made some other trade.

Chevelle waited, watching the idea of his new offer play its way out in Keane's mind. Veil would fight Pitt, and one of them would die. If it were Pitt, Keane's hopes of ruling the court died with him. If it were Veil, he might have a chance, but he'd done his part. He'd captured Ruby and then Grey to keep her under control. And he would have a diary he would have no single use for, because Veil dying meant Pitt had Ruby and the secret—and no use for the actual book.

And Keane had lost.

A long moment, soundless and still, passed. And then

Keane roared, raising a tube to his mouth and firing a poison dart into the crowd. There was an instant of stunned silence ahead of a small, muffled noise as Grey's body landed upon the polished stone floor.

A high-pitched keen rang through the arena as Ruby raised her head to the sky. The ring of trees surrounding the entire clearing ignited in flame.

The sun was falling below the horizon. There were only a few spare moments before the start of the fates' dance. Everyone rose, unsure what the fire fey might do, but it was Liana who spoke. "I challenge you, Keane."

Keane glared at her and threw a slender finger toward the body on the ground. "He is dead. You will never have him, at any price."

"I will fight you for free." Her words were ice, spelled to life with a coldness that resonated sharply against the heat of Ruby's trees.

"And if I win?" he told her, nodding toward Chevelle.

"Yes," she said.

My legs gave way, suddenly and completely. Veil caught my arm, surreptitiously moving me against him. But no one was looking at us. They watched Liana and Keane. Liana owned Chevelle. That had been his bargain, then, himself for me. And now she gambled him in a fight with Keane. For nothing. I let out a helpless breath.

"I accept," Keane said just as the sun dipped into the dark abyss.

Ruby's fire lit the clearing, flickers and flames making shadows dance, bringing the stillness of the stones to life.

Veil wrapped his arm around my waist, throwing his free hand toward the sky. "It is time," he told the eager fey. "The dark night is upon us, and the fates shall dance!"

Lightning and fire rolled through the clouded sky as a

thunderous roar boiled up from the crowd. Rain sprayed onto their outstretched hands, drenching fey and flame alike. A wild wind raged. The clouds parted to moonlight, bright and full and bathing the entire expanse in eerie white and blue. The rain ceased but had wet the floor and key stones, only adding to the unnatural effects. The mass of fey shifted, moving to the center the arena, where the fight would begin.

The dais was positioned perfectly, leaving me able to watch the entire revolting affair. I could see Chevelle as well, strong and poised, his tattered armor laced with black char. Ruby wasn't far behind him, staring dead-eyed at Grey's form on the floor. No one had touched him, not under the threat of her glare. She'd ignited the trees with a purpose, and they knew her power could reach them if they tried anything.

Anvil stood on the outskirts of the masses, his familiar face lit with the paleness of the moon, his expression unswerving. Several score of men stood shoulder to shoulder behind him, the line eventually falling into less formal bands of rogues. Rider stood before those, across the throng from a brother who looked just as battered as he.

Steed, then, was the last missing of my Seven. I'd scarcely had the chance to think of him over the past two days. I hoped he was well. I hoped Thea had stayed with him. I hoped at least he would live.

FLORA AND VIRTUE swooped down to hover at either side of the dais. The contestants' names were drawn, the opening match called. "It begins," Flora said, and the first opponents walked into what, from my angle, was a ring with the standing stones arranged so that two figures could face each other without obstruction. When they did, a tall, thin male wearing ochre robes and carved-bone knives met a stout female with a

190

spear, the bulk of her green-tinted skin layered in a web of vine and jewels. They looked to the sky.

All of us did.

And the sky exploded. The base power rose up through the two of them, conductors for the energy that fought in a ball of blue, violet, pink, and white. It sparked and shone, collided and drew against itself, a sphere of light that desperately struggled to form or shatter, or embrace some other construct than what the two fey held it to. The base power thrummed beneath us, rushing forward through the players to light the atmosphere, and then it detonated, one energy finally overpowering the other so that the winning side remained standing, the losing hit with a blast of power too strong to endure.

The defeated party did not always turn to stone. That fate was reserved for only the strongest matches between only the highest fey. The man in ochre robes ignited, his body burned before our very eyes.

It was not an easy death, but it had been quick.

The next two matches were neither easy nor quick. My stomach had turned and knotted in on itself for so long that it ached. My thirst was nearly unbearable, and the heat radiating off of Veil had me ready to cut the leather arms from my costume. For it was a costume, the garb, the show, all of it to appease the high lord's court. He needed them, but he needed me too. I had agreed to help him with the humans, to save their land—the only place they could use their power—and they would all know he was the only fey I would bargain with, the only one I could trust. I should have let him out of the challenge. I should have let Chevelle bargain the diary against Pitt and ended the whole thing there.

But I couldn't let them win. I had to show power and hold my own, even if it was on fey land. And there was something else, something the fey wouldn't see. The diary was not Ruby's mother's. It had been etched with a V.

I glanced at Chevelle again. He might die at the hands of Keane if Liana lost the battle, but he would have certainly died when Pitt and the others discovered the book was a forgery. I didn't know how long Ruby'd had the plan in play or how for long had the foolish mess been weaving its way toward us all.

"Next match," Virtue shouted into the crowd, "Liana and Keane!"

I probably wouldn't have been the first being to retch on the high court dais, but likely the first elven lord. I pressed it down, my fisted hands bracing against the carved wood of my seat. Veil leaned forward, his breathing slow and his words soft. "It will not be an ending. If she loses, Keane will have to wait until my battle is done."

I would have a moment. As a non-fey, I was not tied to the base power. I would have a small window of time to act, though I had no idea how to do so in the middle of a thousand fey. But Chevelle, my anchor, was there. My magic, tied to him, would be strong enough to fight at least a few high fey.

"Thank you," I said. Veil did not have to offer the advice. I had betrayed him, and I would do it again. He could do the same. "Don't die," I said flatly.

He barked a short and cold laugh. "I cannot."

His realm would be lost. Keane couldn't hold it the way Veil had, and I would be gone and unable to stop the humans from eating away at the base power, the source of their energy, their very lives.

Even the changelings were wrong, because their plan to subvert the use of it could not play out quickly enough to save them. They had too little time. We *all* had too little time.

Liana and Keane walked toward the center stones, covered in blood and littered with ash. Anvil and Rider had brought us an army. We had men from Camber, renowned fighters, and we had rogues, notorious killers. If Liana lived and if Veil lived, we might have a chance. Some of us might make it across the border. But only if they lived.

The earth vibrated beneath us, the crowd's excitement rising with the steady pulse that made its way toward Liana and Keane. Liana grinned, her skin glowing with the power she already held, power that remembered Keane's threat and wanted his blood. Keane's was a darker energy, slithering and foul, but inciting his audience all the more for it. "You will not be stone," she promised him. "I will crush you beneath the sole of my boot. You deserve *nothing* eternal."

Keane screeched, opening himself to the energy and throwing his hands upward so that the base power stuttered, the lull after a massive wave—and just before another hit. Liana stumbled, knocked forward and nearly off her feet. The crowd lurched with her, knowing the disaster it would mean if she didn't immediately join, but she caught herself, her face twisted in anger, her body discolored and dull, melting momentarily into a monstrous reflection of itself before she found her footing and reached to the sky.

Liana's power was glorious, pure white and blinding, her skin losing all semblance of flesh and going iridescent, her lithe frame thinning into something of a blade, and then the energies collided, discharging a flare of heat and sparks that reached us before the concussion of the blast. No one breathed, and then the surrounding fey erupted in chaotic cheers and shrieks. It was what they were waiting on. It was how the base power thrived.

They would be radiant for weeks, overfull and exuberant as they fed on the energy their lands provided. And one of these two fey would have died for it.

I closed my eyes and breathed deeply, feeling every part of

my being. The power inside me was overwrought, and despite it seeming otherwise, my limbs were still intact. It was a good thing, because if Keane won, I would need them. But when the energy finally exploded, releasing the two locked in battle, it was not Keane who remained standing. Liana had kept her word—the other man was silted, spreading across the arena floor. He was smaller than sand and thinner than ash, blowing away with the air. He was nothing.

Veil rose to his feet, not waiting to be called. He inclined his head toward me briefly, and I was unsure if the gesture meant he was confident in his speedy return to my side or that it was pleasant to have known me. I stared at his back, his long wings draping behind a lean, muscled form. He walked into the arena every bit the fey idol they took him for. It silenced the crowd.

Pitt entered the space opposite him, and I was all too aware of the silent forms he'd passed to get there. They were his—Pitt the keeper, the stone maker, the changeling fey who never lost. He would have to lose. If he didn't…

Veil's wings spread wide as he raised his hands skyward, but Pitt only watched, a menacing leer spreading across the changeling's face. Veil tensed, but his back was to me. I could not see his face, did not understand what was happening.

A sudden coldness took over the arena, spreading like frost over glass. The high fey watching became momentarily confused and then agitated, their fury growing with each passing breath. Virtue and Flora were close behind Veil, though I'd not seen them shift to that position. Pitt's hands were spread, his palms up and open to the sky. Veil wasn't moving.

No, I thought, but maybe I'd screamed it, because Chevelle was looking at me, watching as I ran toward the arena, over blood-slicked stone and scattered ash. He was moving, too, and Liana, and a half-dozen other fey. The atmosphere lit with the changeling's magic, and any remaining confusion among the audience cleared.

Pitt had turned Veil's heliotropes against him.

They were preventing him from joining the fight.

Veil would be killed.

FREY

I RUSHED TO VEIL, HIS FIGURE A DARK SHADOW IN THE GLARE OF his opponent's blasting energy. I could see that he was fighting, using everything he had to keep the heliotropes' suggestions at bay, but he'd let them get too close to him. They knew him too well.

He'd trusted a dangerous element.

I slammed into Veil, bracing him as best I could. My magic reached for Chevelle, but he was in the arena, bearing Veil the same as I did. Flora and Virtue were airborne, and we could not reach them with a sword—had I even had possession of one—so I anchored my power through Chevelle and hit them full-force. They reeled, Flora bobbling mid-air and Virtue curling in on herself before shooting toward us at speed. Liana leapt in front of her, knocking the warrior aside, and three other fey piled on, clawing and stabbing and screeching as they went.

The heliotropes' control must have slipped, because Veil's body went rigid, the heat of it singeing my entire side as he became possessed of himself once more. Several fey took flight beside us, tackling Flora in similar fashion, and Chevelle threw himself over me just as the collision of Veil's and Pitt's energies detonated overhead. I was sure Veil had been staggered but could only hope he'd not been badly hurt and that he could win the fight.

Despite Chevelle's cover, the energy was searing, and I moved with him, rolling away from the contest and into the middle of a fey clash. Keane was no longer a threat to me, but Veil had been betrayed, no doubt due at least in some part to his connection to me, and it was impossible to know who else might have been involved. Rider had crossed the court floor and was using an apparently spelled blade to cut the ropes binding Ruby. Fights had broken out throughout the arena, the entire clearing a mass of disorder and madness.

The rogues and soldiers moved forward, circling my Seven and cutting down fey who attempted to break their line. Several high fey took flight, only to be knocked to the ground by the brutal energy radiating from above. The central battle was so intense that I could not stand to look at it—I could only will Veil to come out standing. In the meantime, Chevelle and I got our footing and raced toward Anvil and the others. We'd nearly reached the soldiers' line when an explosion rocked the earth, knocking us from our feet.

My ears rang with a vengeance, every breath a stabbing pain. Men moved around me, but I was hardly aware of who or why. I reached for my knife, any weapon, but there was nothing there. Slick black leather, the costume designed by Veil's fallen fey, met my palm. The present came rushing back to me as Chevelle wrapped a hand around my biceps to jerk me to my feet. We stood, encircled by broken groups of rogues and soldiers from Camber, an injured Rhys, and several unknown fey. We each searched the other, our surroundings, and then farther out to the busted shards of stone that had once been high fey.

"The key stones," someone uttered, their words seeming muffled by the damage done in the recent blast. A figure beside me stepped forward, a thin, blue fey with periwinkle blooms tucked throughout her braids. She stared into the circle, plainly disbelieving what had just happened.

I moved to see past her, seeking out Veil, knowing it had to be him. He had to be the one who survived. But neither man stood.

Bodies lay strewn throughout the arena, rubble and ash coating their skin. Liana rose from across the ring, her form shifting and reshaping until it found itself clean and whole. Two other fey stood near her, stumbling and shaking the dust from their hair. And then a winged shape shifted and rose in the ruined stone.

Gasps echoed from the masses as the fey's wings spread beneath the light of a full moon. It was never a good color for the man—the blue tint lent him a sickly hue.

"Veil," I whispered breathlessly. Relief and dread and utter shock warred at my insides. He shook his wings, and pale dust floated through the dead air. And then a wind blew, mild and sweet and tasting of summer sun.

The crowd began to shift then, slowly and steadily returning with him to life. A gentle rain started and stopped, not scented with poison or the bitter tang of ill intent. I glanced at Chevelle, unsure of our next move. If we were going to run for it, it was time.

He looked toward Liana beneath a lowered brow then back at me. I flicked a glance sideways, indicating Ruby and Grey, but froze there, feeling something fixing me to my place. My mouth came open a fraction, words not falling free. It was impossible, but I was certain: the distant thunder of minds closing in all around. And then, there was the brush of something familiar, someone I knew.

"Junnie," I told him. "She's here."

Chevelle had just enough time to mask his concern before the trees seeped with darkness—black fur, to be precise, though I doubted anyone there had realized that at first. The fey came automatically inward, away from the threat of the unknown. And then understanding dawned, and they moved faster, finding safety beyond the reach of the pack.

Dark-furred wolves spilled through the trees, the moonlight catching the shift of their haunches and the glint of their possessed eyes. Lighter wolves would follow, silver and white, small and large. They took over the clearing, standing at points that no mere animal would find significant. It was the work of an experienced leader, someone who had them firmly under control. It was reminiscent of ordered troops.

Nervous murmurings spread through the court. The fey had never liked dogs. It was an invasion, an infiltration of the worst possible kind.

One of the beasts let loose a growl.

Veil stepped beside me, brushing the dust from his sleeve. "What's this, Lord Freya?"

I shrugged. "Reinforcements."

He looked down at me with a disapproving frown.

I looked up at Junnie and smiled.

33

FREY

Junnie had not come alone. The wolves had been her introduction, and a fine one at that, but she followed the performance with one that shocked even me. Steed had come along with a few dozen castle sentries in tow, including the healer, Thea, and close to fifty of Junnie's new Council guard, scouts and archers, runners and warriors. There were more of them in the forest, I suspected, but she chose to show that many.

She strode toward the court floor, wolves and fey making way as if she were a high lord—and she was, I supposed, at least of a sort. She wasn't simply my Junnie anymore. She was the sole head of Council, poised to take over the entire territory of light elves. I straightened, unsure what exactly she was about. If she had meant to rescue us, we should probably have been getting on our way.

"Freya," she gushed, reaching me and grabbing my hand to squeeze in one of hers. Her greeting was warm, genuine, and so out of place among this high fey battlefield that I simply stared at her in return. She ignored every other being around us—watching us—and smiled. "I am glad to have found you well."

I nodded and cleared my throat.

"I hope we aren't too late," Steed added beside her. He wore a loose shirt with no sign of armor or mail, his sword strapped at an odd angle over his back, but he was alive.

"I believe we were just finishing up here," I told them. "How good of you to come."

Steed flashed a lopsided grin, entirely at ease. "I suppose you'll be wanting this, then." He slid a small wrapped package from a pouch beneath his shirt.

It was warm, not merely from his body heat, and I looked up at him, having no idea what it was for.

"Ruby," he whispered.

Oh. Yes. I laughed abruptly, startling myself and those around me. "Yes," I told him. "This is exactly what I need." I clapped Steed on the shoulder, making him wince but not move away. "Thank you," I said. "Thank you both."

I leaned in, adding softly, "Fetch your sister, please."

I kept hold of Junnie's hand, turning to Veil where he waited at my side. It was a comfort, but it couldn't hurt to present a unified front on our part. "I will stand by my word. The humans will be kept at bay. It will require a nearly full-time residence here, I'm afraid. I will escort my people back to the border, and when they are safely across, I shall return to begin that work."

Veil inclined his head. "We are indebted to your kindness."

"Yes," I told him. "And also to *me*. The challenge completed on my behalf was sabotaged in a willful disregard for your high court laws."

Veil's brows rose, clearly dubious about my claims. He had, after all, been the one sabotaged.

"One of my Seven was killed."

"Oh, he's not dead," Ruby chimed in.

We all turned to her.

She threw a thumb over her shoulder. "Just poisoned. He'll be fine with powdered hickory root and some meadowsweet."

Steed nodded. "Likely have a bear of a headache, though."

"You have a remedy for the toxin?" Veil asked.

"Of course not. It doesn't exist." She shrugged. "I had to poison him for years to build up a tolerance."

Veil stared. Ruby grinned, gesturing toward the parcel in my hands. "I don't suppose that's much help now."

"Actually," I answered, "I'd like to offer it in trade, if you don't mind." I flicked a gaze in my intended target's direction, and she smiled.

"Brilliant."

"Fine, all is settled. Let's get moving before anything else can go wrong."

Junnie squeezed my hand. "One more thing… or two."

She pulled her hand free, stepping back to afford me a better view. At her command, two columns of Council fighters moved forward, splitting their formation to reveal a small human child. *No*, my mind challenged, *not human. It's Isa.*

She was small and thin, but I was no less shocked at her size. She was growing quickly—more at the speed of fey than elf. It was not natural, but little about the girl was. She approached us, staring up at me with big, dark, defiant eyes.

I laughed. "Isa."

She inclined her head politely, a mess of black hair spilling over her eyes. She pushed it back with a petite hand. "I would like to go in your stead to manage the humans."

I stared at Junnie, shocked at the girl's appeal but all too aware of her careful choice of words. She'd volunteered, certainly, but not as favor to me. It was almost as if she meant to lead them.

Junnie's expression was grave, but she said, "She has my blessing in this endeavor. It would mean calamity for you to step away from your throne so quickly after being restored. I know that she seems only a child, but I do not fear for Isa. She has more control over the beings than any of us has yet."

The beings. "You have exposed her to humans?"

Junnie's eyes narrowed on the watching fey. "The changelings have brought several into our lands. I wasn't certain what their intention was before. I'd assumed it was some sort of game. It's clear to me now that they do indeed pose a threat. The draw does not merely affect base magic."

Her words sank in, my exhaustion and addled mind making me take longer than I should have to catch up. "The boundary."

Junnie nodded. The changelings had been sneaking humans out of their forests, bringing them to our lands to destroy protections laid in place by the ancients. But if they could be carried across fey lands, the draw could not be permanent. Magic could be restored once the humans were removed from the scenario. Veil had said they were spreading, describing them like a pestilence. So he must have known that once they'd fully taken an area like the outer forests over, his base magic could not be recovered.

Junnie appeared to have picked up at least bits of my train of thought, for I was confident hers had gone there too. The boundaries could not be left imperfect. They would have to be restored. "Finn and Keaton can assist us on our return," she said.

"Yes," I said shakily, feeling tremendous unease at every new turn. "I think it's time we move now." I glanced at the girl, whose focus was solely on me, waiting for confirmation as if there was no other choice. "I will allow it," I told her, careful of my own words as well. I trusted Junnie's assumption, but I would not forget my mother, the massacre, or what control of that many humans might bring.

Junnie snapped a command at the waiting soldiers, and three more divisions came out of the trees. She eyed the watching fey, daring them to touch her. They would try Isa, I knew. The fey could not be held from a challenge. But she would have Junnie's men and unknown legions of humans, where the base energy could not be kept.

I addressed the watching crowd, letting their high lord beside me hear the threat. "The ancient truce has been broken by both sides. Let this be your warning: we are no longer under treaty. This will be a new arrangement, where you are caged, held in at all sides. The humans will live. The child—Isa —will be in command of them."

Veil hissed, "We had a bargain—"

My look cut him off cold. "You did not specify a time frame. The humans will be held at bay. The fey will be free when they prove they can conduct themselves well."

Veil's eyes went dark, his wings too still. Chevelle's hand slid to his sword hilt.

"We will not be caged." The fey lord's voice was ice, the heat rolling off of him, not so much.

"You already are."

I turned, knowing my Second had my back, and the elven high lord and her guard limped inelegantly off the field.

34

FREY

I STOOD BEFORE THE BALCONY OVERLOOKING THE MOUNTAINS of the North. My home. The stone ledge was not my preferred perch—the fey had stolen that, and I'd nearly been knocked from the rooftop during their previous attack. The haze was thicker there, the view impaired by dark stone walls, but it would do. The cold wind did not cut my eyes or tug at my cloak. It was calm and secure.

We had made it home by the dawn of the second day. Junnie and the others had escorted us the entire route, ensuring that we'd settled in without harm before making their own way home. Grey had been strapped over a horse as Ruby promised each of us he would be fine. Still, she had watched him carefully, her eyes flicking relentlessly from the path to his form. When he was finally taken from the horse, her hands had floated gingerly above his damaged skin, afraid to touch him but clearly yearning to do so. She'd gone into action then, snapping commands and ordering him and the herbs brought to her rooms. No one had seen her since.

The wolves had remained at the border, ensuring that the

207

repaired protections would stay in place. There was a connection between Finn and Keaton that I could never reach, but it appeared that Junnie did not have the same problem. It was something I would give concern to later, though, because there was not energy to focus on it now.

What was important was that we were out of fey lands safely and that, at least on our lands, they were once again at our mercy, even if it was by a tenuous command.

Rumor and revelations spread more quickly than our party, and much of it waited for our arrival home. Pitt's body had not been found, they'd said. Speculation that he'd lived, escaped during the chaos, ran amok. I'd seen the wreckage. I could not imagine that anyone had slipped away. But the fey loved a good legend.

I stood on the balcony, unpinning the silver twine braided through the mess of my hair, and fell silently into the mind of my hawk. We watched from the sky as Chevelle tended to the needs of the castle, drifting above as Steed cared for the horses, as Thea mended Rhys and Rider, as Anvil oversaw repairs. The fey had wreaked havoc on the structure and the general order of things, as usual. They would not be back any time soon.

We'd left Isa to constrict the human encroachment, and by the time we'd parted ways with the girl, I could see where Junnie's confidence came from. The fey had eyed the child with warier gazes than they'd given even the wolves. She might well have been a living keystone. I hoped it worked out. I hoped I wouldn't have to return to do it myself.

"Lord Freya," Liana said from behind me.

I turned from my spot on the balcony, seeing changeling fey in a blue-silk gown. "You should really stop stealing from us."

She nodded. "I come to bid you farewell. For now." She

patted the satchel containing Ruby's mother's diary at her side. I'd been concerned by the trade, unsure if Liana was a harmless enough recipient, but Ruby had promised she'd edited out anything of import, using her mother's powerful signature.

"Thank you," I told Liana, though much of what she'd done had benefitted solely her. "I am glad it was you who survived."

"It could have happened no other way," she told me.

It wasn't true. Keane had been stronger than Liana. But the dance worked like that sometimes. Sometimes, the true superior didn't get to walk away. Sometimes, things worked out.

"And one day, you'll tell me what it was that you wanted with my Second?"

"Unquestionably," she said, drawing the hood of her traveling cloak over her head. "Unquestionably."

LATER, after I'd moved from the balcony up the long corridors and stairs to my room, after I'd washed from my skin the blood and ash, the signs of battle, I found the window of our room. It was a darkening sky, and there was no fear in that for me. Daybreak would come, as it always did, and we would decide how to take on the new trials it offered.

Chevelle's sigh reached me before the sound of his blade being laid on the high table. I had been angry with him, or frustrated, but the exhaustion and the long walk back had taken that out of me. As much as I might want to, I could not hold his choices against him. He had made them long ago, when our circumstances had taken other options away. He might have told me, but it would not have prevented what had come. It would not have saved Ruby.

We had survived, all of us, together.

I let Chevelle clean his battle-weathered skin and have a quiet moment of his own. I took one last look at the sky, one last flight through that dark domain. Stone by stone and day by day, my ancestors had built the castle. They had not all been like Asher—hungry for power, corrupted by greed. Some had been honorable, I was sure. I couldn't say that I remembered their stories, but certainly, they must have been there. History had not been kind to the good men. It had forgotten those who sacrificed without gain.

I didn't need to be remembered. I only wanted to be alive, to stay in the present.

Chevelle's arms wrapped firmly about my waist, drawing me to him. I settled into the embrace, knowing all was well. No matter what was to come, I had Chevelle. We stood among the comforts of our new place, our suite of rooms that held no memorials to the difficulties of our past.

We might look ahead when we were called to, but when we were there, in our room, it would be the only place we were. I would live in Chevelle's arms, feeling the touch of his skin, the sweet sound of him breathing my name, the heat of his lips. It would be my domain.

It would be *ours*, and standing before the window that overlooked the North in Chevelle's embrace, I'd never felt more at home.

EPILOGUE

Ruby

THE FEY HAD DESTROYED NEARLY EVERYTHING RUBY HAD collected. Her stockpile of herbs and tonics had been scattered over the floor of her room and halfway down the hall. The castle staff had cleaned it, carefully separating and disposing of each powder and potion so as not to create something worse. And Ruby sat in Grey's room, balefully staring at his table, where she'd managed to concoct a reasonable medicine or two. She sighed. It would be a long time before she could replenish her stock, and she could manage a much better attitude if she only had some wormroot and aconite to heal Grey's wounds.

She couldn't bear to look at him without wincing. Keane had burned Grey and poisoned him, and it was all her fault.

She flicked a beetle shell off the edge of a fresh mandragora leaf, silently cursing her foolish plan.

"Stop fidgeting," Grey muttered. "It will heal with time."

She rolled her eyes, not looking at him, and his poor burned hand moved to cover hers. His skin was pink and blistered, glowing unnaturally in the candlelight thanks to the salve. She could do nothing more for it but wait.

It was her fault. She'd gotten Grey tangled in the mess. She'd thought she could handle it, that he and Steed would do their part and she would keep her distance, as she always had, to keep them safe.

She hadn't. She'd gotten too close and given too much away, and everyone knew. Everyone had seen how she felt about him, the watching pixies and treacherous little fey. They'd reported it, turned the information over to her enemies without a second thought. Fools, the lot of them. Worse than even her. They'd probably under-bargained, even giving the information away. Those who'd been smart enough to realize what they had probably hadn't made it out alive. The truly clever ones would have stayed on fey lands, never tracking her to the castle.

"Ruby," Grey said, gently moving the pads of his fingers over each of the bones of her hand. "Leave it. What's done is done. We all live."

She shook her head. "No. What's done is *not* done. It never is." She moved to glare at him, but the heat of her anger was stolen instantly at the sight of his face. He was wan, long strands of his hair damp and sticking to his brow from her constant ministrations. Unburnt.

"He left you like that," Ruby told him. "It was his purpose, to allow me to see your face"—she shuddered—"even when the rest of you would be ruined."

"I'm not ruined," he said. "It never got that far."

Keane had planned it, though, Ruby was certain. The high fey had a reputation, and it wasn't good. He would have toyed

212

with his prize for seasons if they'd won her, using Grey for control of Ruby and for their games.

"I should never have allowed you to join us," she decided. "When we stole Frey from the council, you and Steed should have been nowhere in sight."

Grey laughed, but the sound had not come easily. He was still sore and weak. "You act as if you had a choice."

"I had many choices. So many." Her free hand brushed a lock of hair from his temple, slowly and carefully. "I tried to see what was coming, Grey. But I was wrong. Every time."

"Ruby—"

"No. You don't know." She scoffed, and the assembly of candles flickered. She'd not used her magic near Grey, not after what he'd been through. "I've been a fool," she told him. "A solid, thorough fool."

She couldn't heal him more than she had. But she could tell him why he'd been burned. She could do at least that after everything else.

"I won't pretend my motives were pure, at least not to begin with. Chevelle needed something from me, and I from him. It was a bargain, plain as that." She shifted, moving on the edge of the bed to face him fully, where he was propped on an excess of down pillows. "This thing has been hanging over my head the whole of my life, Grey. The fey have wanted to collect me and use me as if I were no more than a stone."

Grey's hand moved over Ruby's, and she let him turn her palm so that it would touch his. She had only ever allowed him that kind of small contact here or there, a tender moment in passing. She had known, deep down, that she could never truly have him, or he her, because of the fey.

"I didn't understand what was at stake," she continued. "Freya, I mean… You saw her." Her free hand gestured vaguely in the air, indicating the broken, bound girl Frey had been. "I didn't think it would go this way, or I might have made another choice." Her gaze rested firmly on Grey's. "I might not have. I think you should know that."

His hand tightened in hers.

"Once we'd rescued her from Council, once we found Asher and saw what he had done… Things changed then for all of us. But Freya took me in. A halfling. A fey in the high guard." She shook her head, still in disbelief. "Don't think I hadn't heard what they thought of fey before that. Don't think their words had never made it to my ears." Grey's eyes were soft, understanding, but he had never behaved as if he knew she had fey blood. To him, Ruby was Ruby. Nothing more. Or maybe *everything* more.

She cleared her throat. "But she took me in. She stood up for me in front of her entire kingdom, above her own men." Ruby hadn't forgotten the banquet, when Freya gave leave for her to claim a price from one of her attendees just for questioning the decision to have a half-fey girl among her guard. Ruby had only taken the man's braid, but it had been enough. It had made her see.

"This is my home now, Grey." She swallowed hard, placing her hand over the cloth that bandaged his arm. "All of this." *Him.* She meant him. She didn't know why she couldn't just say it.

"I was wrong about what Pitt wanted," she explained. "His test. He'd not needed to see if I could harness the base power."

Grey's brow shifted. He'd had enough time to work most of the poison through his system, and Ruby had only given him a mild tonic for pain. His mind worked fine. He understood it was a problem.

"Pitt's motives went deeper. He wasn't the fool I'd thought him." She pressed her lips together. "He wanted to know if I was strong, as strong as my mother." Ruby was stronger. She knew that.

Grey knew it too. She was everything the changeling would need.

"When he disappeared," she began, resisting the urge to look over her shoulder. They were alone there, in the quiet darkness of Grey's suite of rooms. Despite the coldness that ran through her, the changeling fey could not be near. Even if he was alive, even if he'd somehow slipped away. *It was impossible, wasn't it?* Everyone had said it was impossible. *This is your fault*, she reminded herself. "After the fates' dance," she admitted, "when Pitt went missing, he had the ruby." The ruby would have allowed him to store the immense power he would need if he was not in the fey lands.

Grey watched her for a long moment, trying to read the emotions that crossed her face. She barely knew herself. "Ruby, I don't understand. What are you trying to tell me?"

She touched his face, her smooth, pale skin barely grazing his cheek where the shadows danced from candlelight. "*You* are my home now, Grey. I won't risk it. I will not risk any of you."

They were her family, her Seven, and no one could take that from her, not even a changeling fey.

She wouldn't let him. She would find him, even if she had to burn every forest to ash.

Please look for book five in the Frey Saga: *Shadow and Stone*

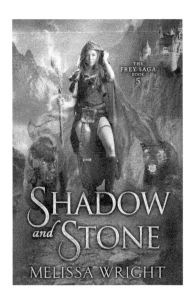

ALSO BY MELISSA WRIGHT

THE FREY SAGA

Frey

Pieces of Eight

Molly (a short story)

Rise of the Seven

Venom and Steel

Shadow and Stone

Feather and Bone

DESCENDANTS SERIES

Bound by Prophecy

Shifting Fate

Reign of Shadows

SHATTERED REALMS

King of Ash and Bone

Queen of Iron and Blood

HAVENWOOD FALLS

Toil and Trouble

BAD MEDICINE

Blood & Brute & Ginger Root

Visit the author on the web at

www.melissa-wright.com

CPSIA information can be obtained
at www.ICGtesting.com
Printed in the USA
LVHW041454150120
643722LV00013B/1011